PEARLS

Philosophies for Living a Robust and Fulfilling Life

GREG TANGHE

Andover,
Minnesota

ISBN 1-931945-10-1

Library of Congress Catalog Number: 2003112784

Printed in the United States of America

First Printing: September 2004

08 07 06 05 04   5 4 3 2 1

Andover,
Minnesota

Expert Publishing, Inc.
14314 Thrush Street NW,
Andover, MN 55304-3330
1-877-755-4966
www.expertpublishinginc.com

To Dar, my wife and soulmate of thirty years. Even after all this time, you still amaze me with your capacity for goodness within. I feel truly blessed to have you as my confidante and best friend. You help make *my* life robust and fulfilling.

CONTENTS

FOREWORD

What if you inherited a machine that was guaranteed to make you happy, but you had no idea how to operate it? Now, if you are like most folks, you'd probably move heaven and earth until you figured out how it worked, wouldn't you?

The fact is, you were *born* with all the resources to make yourself very happy and successful. Unfortunately, you did not arrive equipped with an instruction manual.

It has been left up to you to figure it out. Isn't it strange, then, that most folks don't even bother? They don't read psychology books, they don't take classes or seminars on human behavior, and they don't work with counselors, teachers, or other professionals who could help them make the most of their potential.

Instead, they are content to bump along, not really expecting much out of themselves or of anyone else. Oh, they may go to a lot of trouble to learn to speak Spanish or to scuba dive, but they never take the time to learn how their *mind* works.

Do you suppose this is because no one has ever told them that we are all programmed to achieve happiness and success? It is true. All we have to do is learn to operate the program.

If you want to be happy, you can. Sound simple? Well, it is. But first, you need to educate yourself and learn to control your thoughts.

—Lou Tice, Chairman & Co-Founder
The Pacific Institute, Seattle, Washington

ACKNOWLEDGMENTS

There are many people I need to thank for their patience and understanding as I undertook the writing of this book. My family tops the list; each of you is wonderful and appreciated. Dar, throughout my writing experience, you displayed even more patience with me than usual—*you are extraordinary*.

I thank Carol Dombek, Daniel Bernaciak, and Alan Bolte for helping steer me straight early in my writing. Each of you, in reading my original manuscript, offered invaluable suggestions for improving it. Thank you.

Also, kudos to Sharron and Harry Stockhausen for their great support. Sharron, your fabulous skills in editing provided more expertise than ever expected. After reading your first editing commentary, I knew immediately I obtained the best in the Midwest. You're a tough editor, which makes the job of writing more laborious, and produces winners. This work would have turned out very differently without your guidance. Thank you, Sharron. Harry, you commandeered the procedures of design, setup, production, and all the details of getting my book properly registered. You put it all together so I could tend to my business of writing. Harry and Sharron, I applaud your expertise and whole-heartedly recommend your services to fellow aspiring authors.

A prudent person profits

from personal experience,

a wise one from

the experience of others.

—*Joseph Collins*

A NOTE FROM THE AUTHOR

This book is a recording of some of the truths I discovered in my own life. They are *my* "pearls." There is no expectation that your discovered truths will be, or should be, exactly like the pearls I uncover for myself.

You and I travel different pathways in this life. Each of us chooses our own unique journey, and we encounter different findings along the way. Even when we may occasionally meet at the same place at the same time, you probably discover a truth for yourself that is independent and distinct from what I find for myself.

Our individual observation and comprehension is a part of our diversity and that diverse perspective is a wonderful thing. Through sharing our unique perspectives, I am able to learn from you and you from me.

The more we allow ourselves to understand each other's thinking, the more powerful and effective our own thinking becomes. As one considers and grasps the viewpoint of another, it immediately raises one to a higher plane.

After you finish reading this book, I invite you to share *your* views. I, as the author, would appreciate hearing your introspection and reflection on subjects covered in *Pearls*.

Also, reading the book may bring to mind some additional pearls of your own worthy of passing on to others. Visit the website *www.PearlsBook.com*. The site is a gathering point for discovering the worthy wisdom of others. Our family, our entire family of human brothers and sisters, stands to benefit by sharing unique insights and listening to those of others.

INTRODUCTION

Many people trip and fall through life with little sense of self-direction. They simply allow themselves to wander whichever direction the world will lead them, living impetuously from moment to moment.

They find themselves desiring more, living life in search of happiness. For the most part, they merely endure, as the search continues. Meanwhile, their dreams remain unfulfilled, and therefore their lives unlived.

Your life does not have to, and should not, be lived in search of what only a few discover for themselves. You are worthy of discovering abundant joy for yourself. In fact, you deserve the finest this world offers.

Many people are just a micrometer away from procuring truths that break the shackles binding their lives to mediocrity. They are so very close to experiencing abundant joy, yet rapture and a sense of fulfillment seem just barely out of reach. They find their daily lives mundane, routine, and anything *but* exciting.

So, why do some "get it" as the majority continues to search?

There are no secrets to living a meaningful and joyful life. There are, however, beneficial principles that only a minority of each generation of humanity choose as their own. There are no secrets revealed in this book that are new and fresh to our generation of humanity. The philosophies herein have aided mankind through milleniums of time. Beneficial principles for humanity themselves do not change over time; they have only to be learned by each new generation.

Pearls: Philosophies for Living a Robust and Fulfilling Life is written with the mindfulness that mediocrity is not something *you* need to settle for. You deserve better. *Every* living human being deserves a life greater than a passive commonplace existence.

> **Ain't no man can avoid being born average,
> but there ain't no man got to be common.**
> —*Satchel Paige*

Pearls: Philosophies for Living a Robust and Fulfilling Life shows you the way to gain complete control over the one thing in this world you *can* control. That one thing is how you think—what goes on inside your mind.

This book is a collection of philosophies that, if adopted as your own, will lead you down a path of accepting greater joy in life. Your life will be filled with meaning and a sense of fulfilling purpose.

A note on the structure used in this book:

Use of the English language holds that, when constructing a sentence regarding non-specific gender, male gender pronouns are to be used, i.e., he, him, or his. It is a long-held tradition.

At the same time, back in grade school I was taught that when referring to things of beauty, it is proper to use female gender pronouns, i.e., she, her, or hers.

I regard humanity as the most resplendent of all God's creation, a thing of beauty. The grandeur of human goodness abounds in our daily lives. Mankind is a splendid "invention" by God.

When weighing the merit of God's creation against an antiquated man-made standard for pronoun usage, the scales are lopsided heavily to one side. Because the beauty of humanity holds greater relevance to the subject matter within, throughout this entire book I have opted to use female pronouns in sentences of non-specific gender.

In so doing, no offense is intended toward anyone. Indeed, the opposite is the case.

In this book, there are several quotations from the Bible. For your reference, here is a guide of the various Bible versions used.

DRB – Douay-Rheims Bible
GNT – Good News Translation
GW – GOD'S WORD Translation
KJV – King James Version
NAB – New American Bible
NCV – New Century Version
NRSV – New Revised Standard
RSV – Revised Standard Version
TM – The Message Translation

Those who danced

were thought to be quite insane

by those who

could not hear the music.

—*Angela Monet*

CHAPTER 1

FUNDAMENTAL BELIEFS

There are three basic, but important, beliefs I hold with deep conviction that heavily influence my thoughts and ideas offered in this book. Almost everything I hold of importance in my own life is preempted by these core beliefs. The three beliefs are:

#1 God created man in his image; in the divine image he created him.

—Genesis 1:27 NAB

#2 Life is a daring adventure or nothing at all.

—Helen Keller

#3 There is no security in this world, only opportunity.

—General Douglas MacArthur

#1 – You are Created in God's Likeness

According to Genesis 1:27, in the beginning, God created humans in his own image. That means your ancestors were in his image. And eventually you came to be, likewise, in his image.

What does that mean? Does your Creator have ten toes and ten fingers? And a head full of hair? A stomach that needs filling a couple times a day? And a skeletal and muscle system? Does your Creator have a heart that pumps his blood all day and all night long 24/7? No, somehow I don't think that's it.

I very much doubt the *physical* body is being referred to. God's image is divine. The definition of divine is: like God or of God; sacred; holy.

Wow!! That sounds like heady stuff I'm implying here! You may be thinking, "Me!!?? Holy or sacred? Divine!!??"

On the surface, the Biblical statement appears to imply that humankind has been granted Divine authority. But, what does it really mean?

God further explained in Gen. 3:22 NAB by stating, "See! The man has become one of us, knowing what is good and what is bad!" I believe the passages of Gen. 1:27 and Gen. 3:22 mean God created you with the ability to think, to reason, to differentiate between what is good and what is not so good. He designed creative ability in you coupled with a predominant desire to do good. Additionally, you are granted freedom to choose how to use all of it—how to think and how to act.

The greatest gift which God in his bounty bestowed in creating, and the most conformed to his own goodness... was the freedom of the will.

—*Dante Alighieri (1265-1321)*

These characteristics are all qualities of his, and your divine nature.

I surely do not mean to imply you are as great as the One who created you. God has ability to create earth, natural light, the air we breathe, and life itself from nothingness, whereas you, as a mere human being, create only lesser things of a finite nature. You accomplish creativity through thought impulses and *bodily* action. Bear in mind, no matter how great your mental composition, you are still merely a member of humanity who will always be lesser than God.

You and I, as God's human creatures, hold dominion over other animal life (Gen. 1:28). Each of us is obligated, by our status of advantage, to uphold a quality existence for all earthly life.

You help create a better earthly existence through the use of your brain, your thinking, and your doing. Your Creator put a model of the finest processing equipment *ever built* right into your head, covering it with a thick encasement of protective armor. God evidently feels your thinking is (and therefore you are) of vital importance to his plan.

Your mind, and what goes on in that semi-organized mass of gel in your head, is the very essence of who you are. You *are* what you think.

People are Good

People have been contrived by God as good creatures with a basic desire to do that which is right and good. That is the very reason you get a warm, fuzzy feeling inside when you perform good deeds. And it is also why you feel guilt or shame when you sin, or assent to a dishonorable thought or act.

Evil occurrences are unusual occurrences. It is *because* people are mostly good that our newspaper articles and radio and television newscasts are generally of a negative nature. Good happenings, because they *are* the norm, are not newsworthy.

> **Goodness is uneventful.**
> —*David Grayson*

Consider the following newscast. "Sally got a B+ on her history test. The rain helped Mary's garden grow faster today. Bill and Cindy had a wonderful time dining and taking in the opera performance last evening. Charlie sang in the church choir on Sunday."

Who would watch *that* newscast? It's not news; these good things happen all the time.

People *are* good!

> **The everyday kindness of the back roads**
> **more than makes up for**
> **the acts of greed in the headlines.**
> —*Charles Kuralt*
> *in* On the Road With Charles Kuralt

It seemed to me my father grew wiser and more positive with age. As he was dying from cancer a few years ago, my father offered inspiration to me.

A couple weeks before his death, he was quite weak and could barely, even with assistance, get on his feet. That particular day, as he was taking a very slow shuffling walk in the hall of the nursing home, I walked alongside holding one arm as his sister helped steady my father by holding his other arm.

I was so proud of him when he said very weakly, "Ya know? It's still a pretty good world, isn't it?"

I was dumb-struck! My thought was "life doesn't get much worse than this," and my father was still witnessing the goodness of this earthly life! He chose to focus on the good in most people rather than the evil doings of a few.

He was a wise man. It is my hope that I may be as focused on the goodness of God's earthly creation days before my departure from this world.

We all have good and bad within us. But people *are* good most of the time. The huge majority of us are not making the negative newscasts, and never will.

#2 – Life is a Daring Adventure

Is every moment in your life of value?

Is every day in someone's life important?

Is every life significant?

I remember a few decades ago seeing on television a long, long line of Ethiopian people standing out in the baking sun waiting for a handout of raw grain so they could eat. Eating is a pretty basic need.

I saw lines of thin emaciated, pot-bellied bodies that were naked or nearly naked. As the cameras rolled from face to lifeless face, the thing forever etched in my mind is these people had flies crawling on their bodies and faces. The people were too weak and exhausted to even shoo the flies off their bodies for comfort.

It struck me that our pets and livestock here in America were living more robust and happy lives than those humans! In these people's state of extreme poverty, it was unlikely there would be any money available for formal education of any kind. A hopeless situation.

Contrast the situation of these starving people with your own circumstances right now. Doesn't it make you want to jump with joy that you are so blessed today? To scream out to whomever is within earshot, "Yeah, life is great! What a gift I have been offered. I'll never squander another moment, never, ever again. Life is too precious, too short. I can't get enough of it!"?

> **If you were fully appreciative
> of just one-tenth of your blessings,
> it would cause you to spring to life
> with such exuberance that
> nothing would stop you.**
> —*Ralph S. Marston, Jr.*

But the predominant outlook you hold is likely somewhere between a state of total listlessness and one of enthusiastic gratitude. As a repayment to the One who gave you the gift, shouldn't you be absolutely exhilarated about your life? Your Creator could have picked any sperm and any egg to make new life. But he chose you. The ultimate gift was given to *you*!

What are you going to do with his generous grant? Please don't tell him he picked the wrong embryo. Your Creator gave this world a magnificent gift in choosing you. Yes, he did!

**Fear not that thy life shall come to an end,
but rather fear that it shall
never have a beginning.**

—*John Henry Cardinal Newman*

I dare you to become the spirited and vivacious person just described. I challenge you to make *your* life worthy! I challenge you to, within the first five minutes of each day, thank your Creator for this wonderful day, this brand new and exciting opportunity to make the world a more joyful and happier place. Are you living your life as joyously as you can? If not, why not? Life is a colossal gift from your Creator. Strive to live up to his expectations! Have fun in this venture of living!

Life is a daring adventure or nothing at all.

#3 – There is No Security in this World

There are few things in this world that can be counted on with 100 percent certainty. Indeed, you are unable to predict even *your very own* behavior with that kind of accuracy.

And about the time you think you have something figured out for sure, a shift occurs. Things change all the time.

All conditions, whether presently in a state of complacency, chaos, or somewhere in between, are subject to the unpredictability of luck, continual change, and natural dynamics. This intrinsic condition of perpetual unpredictability in our lives deprives the human mind of any lasting sense of security.

In fact, there is no security in this world, only opportunity.

Life is for Living

Many choose to live their own lives through the activity of others. They listen to, or maybe even spread, gossip about others. Or they can hardly wait to get off work so they can get home, have a quick meal, and do what they do best. Unfortunately for many, what they do best is not to live, but to watch *other*s live.

They watch those who make the news, they watch those who broadcast the news, or the talk show host and her famous guests, or sports players. They watch actors and actresses as they perform in a movie or television sitcom, or they watch the activities of people involved in what is referred to as reality television. Perhaps their attention is directed toward the counsel offered in horoscopes or the newspaper advice column. It matters little if the people being watched are real life or merely performing for entertainment.

> **People have the chance to live,
> but they spend most of their time
> living through others.**
> —*John F. Groom*

Rather than living their own life, many choose the lifestyle of being a couch potato or a fan in the stands living vicariously through the lives of others. What joy is in that?

Get a life of your very own and live it. Take an *active* role in *your* life!

Life is a daring adventure or nothing at all.

We choose which thoughts we let reside in our minds. We choose for ourselves whether to think positive growth-producing or negative self-limiting thoughts. By choosing our thoughts, each of us gets what we want out of this earthly life.

Choose to enhance your life by getting excited about possibilities. Experience for yourself the same excitement a child feels when undertaking a new venture. Grasp the same exhilaration a sports participant or a risk-taker feels as they perform to their full capability. When your mind takes you to a place that would not be in your "comfort zone," go there for real; challenge your inner complacency. Why simply watch others live out *your* fantasies? Take a chance on experiencing the exhilaration for yourself.

Leave little time for boredom in your life. Accepting a boring life is an insult. It is a cold shoulder "no thank you" rebuff to your Creator. And it is also insulting to your *own* distinction as a person of dignity and worth.

What we are is God's gift to us.
What we become is our gift to God.
—Eleanor Powell

The three predominant thoughts outlined in this chapter will be referred to often in the remainder of this book. They support definition to all else I think.

CHAPTER 2

CHANGE

You have probably heard there are two certainties in this world: death and taxes. There is a third one: change.

Change can often be a scary concept for people since change alters the current condition. Unless the current condition is painful (sometimes, even *if* the current condition is painful), we develop a bond with its familiarity. Because the current condition is what is known, we develop an acclimation to its presence and generally feel some discomfort in letting it go.

We shrink from change.
Yet is there anything that
can come into being without it?
—Marcus Aurelius, 121-180 A.D.

Change is *always* occurring. It cannot be avoided. Change is constant and unending. In this very moment while reading this sentence, change is going on in your head. Your mind is processing the information you read and either storing it in the acceptance file or discarding it into the waste file. If the idea you are reading is not new to you and is already stored in the save file of your mind, then you may be experiencing change through acknowledgment of the already existing idea with a greater sense of certainty.

Change is going on in your physical world as well. The physical world is a recurring order of growth and decay. The seed of a plant germinates, develops into a seedling, grows to eventual maturity, dies, and then rots. The life process of the animal kingdom follows the same cycle—continual change.

Your cells are dying and replenishing themselves at this very moment as you read. Your heart is re-circulating the blood throughout your body to feed all your body's cells. Your lungs are bringing in new fresh air and exhaling de-oxygenated air.

You are constantly being re-invented at all times, every moment, even as you sleep, daydream, work, or rest. You are what you think and even *that* is ever-changing.

Hey, that's exciting! That means that at any moment, you can start over. In fact, at every moment you *are* starting over, getting a fresh new start.

> **...anyone can start from now**
> **and make a brand new ending.**
> —*Carl Bard*

One year from now you will be a new person, guaranteed. And the good news is YOU get to pick which direction you will go. Of course, you cannot choose everything that will come your way, but you certainly can point your direction. You can (and do) choose what your reaction to every action will be. You also choose whether any action is, or even has previously been, a positive or negative experience for you.

There are many times when it will be almost impossible to see, but always remember: there is something good in everything that is bad. There is *some* good able to come out of the situation. You will benefit by learning to seek out the good and focusing on it. The amount of good is not always proportionate to the amount of bad, but it often can be. An example: many people lose their security blanket, i.e., their job and their steady paycheck. How often have you heard six months after the fact, "It was the best thing that could have happened to me. I just didn't realize it at the time."? Having the blanket pulled out from under her forces the complacent worker to search for new opportunities.

Your Past was a Recital

Your past was a recital for today.

Your past successes and your past mistakes do not exist. They are no more. All that remains are the memories and the lessons that came with those experiences. The memories, the lessons, and your current perception are each a part of *the present situation* for you—and the present situation, the current condition, is all you have.

Your past experiences also result in a reputation perceived through the eyes of others. Whether you appreciate or dislike their perceived reputation of you, it is wise to keep in mind how others have chosen to estimate your character *is* from your past.

Your character is continually forming. As your thoughts change, your character changes accordingly. The reputation (of your past) others hold of you may, or may not, be truly indicative of your character at this time, if indeed it *ever* was.

We can alter our life by altering our thoughts.
—*Wayne Pickering*

With time, your present reputation, whether you feel it is good or bad, will fade and gradually be replaced with your new image.

A Business Lesson

Large companies today invest massive amounts of time and money conducting research for new product development. They make an effort to be innovative in coming up with the next great idea or product. Innovative companies take change by the hand and give it direction. Like it or not, innovators and inventors influence direction in *your* life. No doubt, some inventions, such as the automobile and the electric light bulb, have dramatically influenced your lifestyle.

Why are innovators doing all this? Is it worth it? Obviously, *they* think so; they expect to gain by researching new ideas. Prosperous businesses realize change continually happens, and they choose to do something about it.

**It's not the strongest
of the species that survive,
nor the most intelligent,
but the one
most responsive to change.**
—*Charles Darwin*

Rather than fight the futile battle of trying to avoid change, successful companies choose to point the direction of change. They purposely position themselves in the direction of growth. Decision-makers of flourishing companies realize when a company discontinues growth and new development, it begins its journey toward death.

We, as individuals, can take a lesson from this meaningful practice of successful enterprising. We need to invest in our *personal* growth. Growth of self happens through learning and thinking anew. We need to accept, and even welcome, change in our being.

When you're through changing, you're through.
—Bruce Barton

Some people take technical and college courses, or continue to learn in other ways, when they are in their seventies, eighties, and even nineties. Others, amazingly, feel they "know it all" by the time they have reached their teens or twenties.

When we discontinue learning, or when we have decided we are one of those who knows most of the answers, we are no longer able to hold an open mind toward the ideas and reflections of others. When a person loses her zeal for new learning or for helping others, she makes a turn in her life from growth to diminishment. It is the point in one's life of being "old" and can happen at almost any chronological age. The number of years since birth holds little relevance.

**Nobody grows old merely
by living a number of years.
We grow old by deserting our ideals.**
—Samuel Ullman

My wish for you is that *your* time of diminishment begins when you are on your deathbed and not before. But—the choice is yours.

CHAPTER 3

TRUTH & DESIRE TO BE RIGHT

Truth is absolute and unconditional. Real truth is correct and genuine, regardless of whether or not people perceive it correctly. What people believe to be true in their own minds may or may not be actual truth. To differentiate the two, throughout the remainder of this book, I will refer to actual truth as truth, without quotation marks, and what people *perceive* to be reality in their own mind will be "truth," contained within quotation marks.

"Truth" is conditional. "Truth" may or may not have any resemblance to what actual truth is. For example, once upon a time, our world was flat. Since everyone could see the earth was *obviously* flat, that "truth" was in the minds of every living being. That "truth" eventually changed into what virtually everyone regards as being real truth today—the world is *not* a flat surface but actually is a huge round sphere. Sometimes "truths" that are not truth in actuality may exist in the minds of virtually *every* human being, as in the example just cited.

Accepted "truths" may vary from individual to individual. The numerous variations of religious followings are an example of "truth" varying between individuals. There are several major religions of the world. Most, or all, of the major religions now have factions that have split off from their original dogma to form yet another religious faith. And each of those religions has some followers who choose, as individuals, to believe certain ideas even though the beliefs deviate from their religion's central doctrine. Since there is such great variety in what is regarded as religious truth in the minds of all humanity, it is quite obvious the "truths" of all religious conviction cannot be *actual* truth.

Each of us judges for ourselves what is accurate information and what is false information. Once you decide a certain condition to be correct in your mind, it becomes your "truth."

Our Desire To Be Right

One of our most prevalent weaknesses as humans is an innate need to be viewed as being right or correct in our thinking. We want to be revered as the smart one. We enjoy the moment when someone points out that we are correct in our thinking, especially if a circle of friends may be present to witness our prowess.

Your desire to be viewed as being correct is ego driven. The desire to be seen as being right in the eyes of your peers can be so strong, it may even taint the "truth" you paint in your *own* mindset. That's when your "reality" may not, in fact, be realistic.

By letting go of your own ego, you enable yourself to better relate to another person's perspective, thereby advancing your own level of understanding.

**The need to be right—
the sign of a vulgar mind.**
—*Albert Camus*

I know a gentleman who enjoys the hobby of trading commodity futures. One spring, for whatever reason, he expected the price of soybeans to rise sometime the following summer. He had, in fact, bet on such occurrence by purchasing August soybean call options. If he were indeed correct in his assumption of a price increase, owning the call options would give him the right to buy soybeans at a relatively low price, thus allowing him to profit from the transaction. But, if he were to gain monetarily on this venture, it all had to happen *before* a certain expiration date. In relating this experience, the gentleman explained to me that immediately *after* the August calls had expired worthless, and he had lost his entire investment, the price of soybeans did indeed rise. His rationale was, "I was right. They just went up too late."

In many aspects of life, timing is important. If your timing is wrong, then you are wrong. In this particular instance, timing *was everything*. The person who bought the time-sensitive options was not able to admit he was wrong in his assumption and even found the need to point out he was, in fact, correct.

If he was right, then the party who sold the call options to him must have been wrong. But she wasn't. She won the bet and was rewarded with financial gain.

Rather than trying to satisfy your compulsive need to be right, seek truth, no matter how unpalatable it may be. Truth is unbiased and always correct. Instead of lazily allowing your brain filter to accept only what is in agreement with what you *already* believe, you can gain greater understanding through receiving new input more objectively. By learning to accept and understand a particular truth for what it truly is, your mind will advance to the next level of understanding. That is better than being "right."

> **Truth is like the sun.**
> **You can shut it out for a time,**
> **but it's not going to go away.**
> —*Elvis Presley*

Timing is Everything

There is a wise gentleman who had proverbial words for me to consider. He told me, "If you think about it, you can make money at anything. It's all in the timing." I was young at the time and did not grasp the full meaning of what was being said.

I have eventually come to find his statement to be true on more occasions than I care to admit.

I will recount one such occasion here. In 1980, I made an impulsive financial investment.

At the time, each day on the news we heard the price of gold was sky rocketing. Virtually every day, it seemed, the price of gold closed at a higher price than the day before. In fact, usually at a much higher price. I didn't think much about it until one evening when I was talking on the phone to my older, and wiser, brother.

My brother boasted he was the proud owner of several Kruggerand gold pieces. In fact, he bought them at a comparatively low price several months earlier. I had no idea; I was both surprised by it and envious of his good fortune!

I, who a few minutes earlier was not the least bit concerned with the trend of gold prices, suddenly decided I wanted to be in on the action. My brother agreed to sell four of his gold coins, which depleted my wife's and my entire savings account. When I asked him if he thought it was a good idea, he chuckled and said, "Would I be selling if I thought it was a good idea to be buying?"

Undeterred, I snatched them up. I wanted them; he shouldn't have *all* the fun.

Well, you may be able to guess what happened. The very next day, the price of gold hit what is still today the all time historic high.

Since that time, I have learned when the very last person buys, i.e., the person who has never in her wildest dreams considered buying (that would be me, in this case), there are no more buyers left, and the market is at its peak. Well, it was a classic top; the last person bought.

What the wise do in the beginning, fools do in the end.
—Warren Buffett

Several months later, I swallowed my pride, went down, and cashed in on what value was left in my gold Kruggerands.

I once considered that transaction to be my very first financial investment that suffered a loss. In retrospect, I now realize it was my very first speculative trade.

Some years later, I informed my spouse that I was once again considering buying gold as a speculative investment. She was very quick to point out I should have learned something from the first time I tried it, and she didn't think it was very wise for me to be trying it again.

I assured her I had indeed learned lessons through my earlier experience. I learned gold can be a risky speculative investment. Who would argue with that? However, the lesson I chose to focus on, and still do today, is that timing, along with risk management, is everything.

I honestly do not recall if I made my second gold purchase at that time or not. And that is not important. The important thing is the lesson that I learned.

The Majority is Wrong the Majority of the Time

While still in high school, I heard the phrase *the majority is wrong the majority of the time* from one of my teachers. It's a lesson that stuck with me and has served me well.

We like to do what everybody else deems to be acceptable, don't we? We tend to follow the crowd. If everybody's doing it, it can't be too bad, right? Wrong!

> **Whenever you find yourself on the side of the majority, it is time to pause and reflect.**
> —*Mark Twain*

It is all right to pay attention to conventional wisdom as long as you recognize and understand *conventional* wisdom is exactly what you are paying attention to. With conventional wisdom, you have acquired the knowledge the masses already possess, which is the very reason it is referred to as "common" sense. That in itself should give you some idea as to the usefulness of the information. Generally, common knowledge is of limited value.

Do your own analysis. Be different when conditions warrant being different from the rest of the pack. Contrary thinking will very often pay.

> **Truth does not become more true
> by virtue of the fact
> that the entire world agrees with it,
> nor less so even if
> the whole world disagrees with it.**
> —*Maimonides*

When the majority is buying, you should consider selling. When the majority is selling, buy. It takes courage to fly in the face of common sense but, more times than not, you will benefit. Herd mentality is dangerous! Sense is not really such a common thing; however, common sense *is*.

Abiding by popular opinion is generally not a safe or secure principle for you to adopt. Contrary thinking not only works with your dollars in the markets, it works in almost all disciplines of life.

Great Ideas are Delicate

A desire, dream, or new idea in its infancy is an extremely delicate thing. In the early stages, one's dream can be easily wiped out by a joke, a smirk, or the raise of an eyebrow. If you wish for your desire to grow and become reality, endear your new thought with some degree of resolve before disclosure to outside influence.

A small idea is easily envisioned, and therefore already nearer fulfillment than a grand idea. The more noble your thought, the more delicate its condition in infancy.

> **Don't worry about people stealing your ideas.**
> **If your ideas are any good**
> **you'll have to ram them down people's throats.**
>
> —*Howard Aiken*

Accept Advice with Caution

In doing analysis of situations, be careful where you look for advice. Be leery of accepting an "expert's" counsel with unabated sureness.

Certainly there are people in any field or industry who may have greater insight than the majority of us. However, do not forget those regarded as experts are still fallible human beings. Like everyone, they make mistakes too. You will have to judge for yourself whether someone qualifies in being expert enough to advise you in your particular situation.

Consider the following examples[1]:

- William Everett, who ran the U.S. Patent Office in the early part of the last century, claimed he would soon have to close up shop because "everything had already been invented."

- In 1911, France's top military Commander, Marshal Foch, said, "Airplanes are interesting toys, but are of no military use."

- In 1943, IBM Chairman Thomas J. Watson said, "I think there's a world market for about five computers."

- In 1946, Daryl F. Zanuck, head of the Twentieth Century Fox Film Studio, said, "TV won't be able to hold on to any market. People will soon get tired of staring at a plywood box."

- In 1962, Decca Recording Company rejected the Beatles with the words, "We don't like their sound and guitar music is on the way out."

Oh really?

All these respected men and businesses were considered to be at or near the top of their industry. They were revered among their colleagues. I suspect most people would have considered them to be experts in their field.

These people may have been more knowledgeable than others. Whether they qualified as experts or not is up to the discretion of the person doing the analyzing.

We *all* have much to learn yet. Even the top dogs.

Pick Your Fights

Warning! Fighting may be hazardous to your health. Pick your fights carefully.

It takes two to have a fight. Whether or not you start it, if you allow yourself to be part of a fight, you are guilty.

If you "know" you are right and the other person is wrong, isn't that good enough? Why does the other person have to see things in the same way you do? You know you are right. And she thinks she is right. There is no harm in letting her think that. It is not *necessary* for the rest of the world to know you are right. Potential disturbance dismissed, now move along and refocus your energy on bigger and better things for yourself.

> **Maturity begins when we're content to**
> **feel we're right about something**
> **without feeling the necessity**
> **to prove someone else wrong.**
> —*Sydney J. Harris*

Of course, there are exceptional instances where standing up to others *is* in the best interest of all. That is understood, however rare those instances may be.

If you have sense to generally view life in the big picture, you find a reservoir of patience. There are few markedly significant moments in most people's lives. By taking the big view, you recognize most moments in life *are* small and relatively insignificant.

Don't sweat all the little stuff. Life's too short for that. Especially if you intend to have fun with your life.

Most fights are not worth fighting. Certainly there are times when you simply should not allow yourself or someone else to be picked on, but in *most* cases, you are better off simply looking the other way.

When someone chooses to criticize you, your best response is not a retaliation of your own. Confrontation immediately closes a door to open-minded dialogue and positive possibilities.

If you are of disposition composed enough and wise enough, step back and take your ego out of the picture. Look objectively at the accusation being directed toward you.

What is the other party actually saying? Where did the accusation come from? Why did she say it? Is the accusation true? Seek genuine, and as much as possible, unbiased, understanding of the situation. Tolerance for the opposing party's view, and a solution to the disagreement, can be most easily acquired through mutual understanding. By observing her thought in an objective way and *understanding why* she feels the way she does, you can present a more constructive response to what possibly could have blown up into an argument or perhaps even a brawl.

When two people fight, whether physically or verbally, both parties *always* lose. When you fight with someone, the display of offensive character is a reflection not only of the party you are fighting with but each of you. When the quarrel is over, even if you feel you came out on top, realize you have lowered yourself to become a smaller person for the antagonism.

> **In taking revenge,**
> **a man is but even with his enemy;**
> **but in passing over,**
> **he is superior.**
>
> —*Sir Francis Bacon*

There is no good that comes from burning your bridges through conflict. Spare the antagonistic relationship.

Sometimes when a bitter battle is involved, such as can often happen in a divorce scenario, your vindictiveness begins to eat at your own health. Not only does the hostility cost your former lover, it will do even *greater* harm to you.

> **Resentment is like drinking poison**
> **and waiting for the other person to die.**
>
> —*Carrie Fisher*

Forgive past transgressions and let your bitterness go. Granted, when you feel someone has misused you, it is not an easy feat to forgive that person. But you *must* forgive for your own good. The act of forgiving will benefit *you* more than it will benefit your adversary. Hatred is a malignancy with far-reaching effects on your overall health. Holding bitterness and hatred inside afflicts you physically, emotionally, and mentally.

> **The heaviest thing you carry**
> **through this life**
> **is a grudge.**
> —*Author Unknown*

Imagine how it would feel to be free of this weight that's dragging you down day after day. By ridding yourself of resentment and hatred, you free yourself to experience life with renewed energy. Your mind and your refreshed thinking experience a new spirit that empowers you and enables you to move forward.

Ridding your mind of bitterness and hatred toward another involves a two-step process.

Owning up to *your own responsibility* is important in forgiving others. Realizing it takes two to have a disagreement, recognize *your* role. In order to rid yourself of feeling hatred or resentment toward someone, you must first recognize how *you* mishandled the relationship, then forgive yourself. Only by freeing (and enabling) yourself can you allow forgiveness of the other person. Do not merely try to forget the transgression; forgive the *person* who wronged you.

As long as you choose to hold an unforgiving thought toward your transgressor, he or she holds authority over your ability to find wholly fulfilling joy. It is a choice, *your* choice, whether you hold this burden or rid yourself of it once and forever. Free yourself, and instead direct your energy toward what can be beneficial for you.

One of the most lasting pleasures you can experience is the feeling that comes over you when you genuinely forgive an enemy.
—*O. A. Battista*

Let Go

When you hang onto your need to be right, your need for self-importance, your need for revenge, indeed your need for anything, you secure a ball-and-chain to yourself that follows you wherever you go. The restraint is slowing you down, preventing you from discovering the potential for greatness you were designed with at birth. When you discover your ability to release your own ego, you gain a whole new freedom and become better equipped to attain a healthy outlook on life.

When I let go of what I am, I become what I might be.
—*Lao-Tzu, 6ᵗʰ century B.C.*

You don't *need* to win an argument, you don't *need* a fancy car to show your affluence, you don't *need* to show another individual you can do a particular thing yourself and in your own way. These are all ego-driven "unnecessary needs" that restrain someone from growth and personal fulfillment. Learn to let go.

There is a peaceful wisdom that comes through resigning oneself to inevitable death. In that circumstance, a person is essentially forced to let go of her personal ego and to let God take over. Such condition is the epitome of letting go.

When you are truly able to resign your ego, to let go, your realization comes to light as to what is important and what is only fluff in this world. Love gains a new prominence and material possessions lose their value.

Prejudice and Love

Prejudice means to *pre-judge* someone or something.

Is it fair to pre-judge anyone? Well, no, it isn't. But, in actuality, each and every one of us is guilty of pre-judging and prejudice.

When we see a neatly coifed man dressed in a smartly tailored business suit and shiny polished shoes or a young man with long, unruly, greasy hair and tattered, soiled clothing complete with plenty of arm tattoos, we instantly make some presumptions about each of them. We can't help it. We have been conditioned by past experience.

That type of prejudice is damaging enough. However, there is a far more hurtful form of prejudice out there, one that has nothing to do with how one has chosen to tailor or groom themselves.

When a person judges another, not as an individual, but as one of an entire class of people, then she is being unfair to both herself and that individual. I am referring to when a person has contempt or hatred for another person without knowing anything about her except her skin color or her gender or her religion or her approximate age.

A person must have a profoundly small or deranged mind if she is of character able to convince herself she is superior to an entire sect or race of humanity. No person could ever live up to such a claim, least of all the person with a mind capable of such thinking.

Love one another
as I have loved you.
—John 15:12 KJV

Isn't it refreshing when you meet a stranger who seems to have a genuine feeling of goodwill toward you? Even though that person doesn't know you, she seems to appreciate you as a person. Because of her friendly and personable nature, you sense an instinctive human camaraderie with her.

That is love, the opposite of prejudice. It takes a robust and healthy mindset to acquire that sort of benevolent feeling toward an unfamiliar fellow human. When you are able to experience selfless spiritual love of other humanity, rather than fear, hatred, or discrimination, you yourself automatically acquire a higher sovereignty. Part of the joy of bearing a benevolent love toward others is the more you feel and express love, the more love from others comes back *toward* you.

No person will experience a consummate joy of living without knowing at least some level of that kind of love. What a vastly different world this would be if everyone were to develop love and eliminate prejudice in her own mind!

> **There are in the end three things that last:**
> **faith, hope, and love,**
> **and the greatest of these is love.**
> —*1 Corinthians 13:13 NAB*

Each person who is chosen by our Creator to live here on earth is unique, no matter their race, gender, or any other condition. We can, if we allow ourselves, learn from the insights of each other.

Human diversity is a creation by the Master Creator and all will benefit by regarding this diversity as a *gift* to humanity. How dare any of us misuse our Creator's goodwill through prejudicial thinking? Rather, we should be celebrating our good fortune. What a unique and useful largess we have received!

> **If the human race is to survive**
> **and fulfill its destiny,**
> **we must finally accept the fact that**
> **diversity is part of humanity's heritage.**
> —*Stan Lee*

Each society from all countries of the world has strengths to offer the rest of humanity. We are all in this together as human siblings. We benefit through understanding each other's cultures, customs, and traditions.

Let us celebrate our diversity!

CHAPTER 4

HABITS

A habit requires no effort. A habit, being an automatic action for you, can become an integral part of who *you* are. Since you and your habits are tightly intertwined, it is wise to develop your habits judiciously and purposely, rather than simply leave their creation to indiscriminate chance.

We form our habits, then our habits form us. I first heard this wise adage many years ago. It is simple, but profound.

Our unseized time flows toward our weakness.
—*Gordon MacDonald*

It becomes more rewarding to purposely develop a healthy habit for yourself than to haphazardly acquire a negative habit that becomes a hindrance to you. Once you encumber yourself with a negative habit, it takes greater effort to rid your mindset of that unwanted automatic impulse and to replace it with another more desirable habit. Many people spend the majority of their lives nail-biting, smoking cigarettes, overeating, or using hurtful language; the list of nasty habits goes on and on. Virtually everyone adopts some habit that can annoy even *themselves*. Then, they desire change or correction of the unwanted habit.

Habits are first cobwebs, then cables.

—Spanish proverb

The truth is, you can break any habit. Once a habit becomes established as an automatic action for you, it requires much effort to undo, but realize you are not obligated to own the unwanted habit. Ownership is a choice, just as letting go is a choice.

If you want change in your life, it is very important you possess both *strong desire* for change and *belief* you will succeed. Without strong desire and expectant belief backing the effort, there will be no change, at least not change of any enduring nature. You may be able to modify your behavior for a short while, but unless you create new thinking on the inside, with time, your old habitual self is sure to resurface.

Once you undertake an effort in search of change, persist in seeing your transformation through to successful completion. Otherwise the entire effort not only becomes a waste of your time and energy, the *failure* of the effort reinforces any emotions of self-insufficiency you may already be feeling. Your subconscious mind accepts your failed attempt at face value. That only worsens the situation, making your transformation ever more difficult to accomplish in a possible future attempt.

Develop a Disease-Resistant Healthy Mind

Bearing in mind what you think is what you are, a healthy mind is a healthy you. Your mind works similarly to the working of a computer. If quality programming and quality data go in, quality results come out. Or conversely, garbage in, garbage out.

Whoever came up with the quip "you are what you eat" must have been referring to the mind rather than the body. The adage is certainly more relevant to our mental being than our physical being.

In this book, I focus on the concept of quality thinking. However, you will benefit by knowing some characteristics of unhealthy thinking. I refer to the various conditions of negativity in your mind as your "self-sabotaging mental diseases." Each of us encounters these energy-draining diseases at times. Of course, just as with physical diseases, you will benefit by overcoming your diseases of the mind as rapidly and painlessly as possible.

These self-sabotaging mental diseases, some of which I identify in this section, gain dominance in an unhealthy mindset.

Look at Life in the Big Picture

If you take care of the big things, the little things take care of themselves. That runs counter to what you have likely heard in the past. *Consequential* matters are far more worth your time and effort than the relatively negligible details of life. The little moments, the little details are merely an extension of your overall picture.

What to order off the menu? Which hair rinse should I purchase? Should I wear this pair of shoes today or that pair? These are relatively inconsequential everyday decisions. Some people overburden themselves with "analysis paralysis" of such everyday decisions.

Little things affect little minds.
—*Benjamin Disraeli*

When I was working for a retail store, I offered to help a customer who appeared to be a college student. She was busy perusing writing pens for the longest time, so I assumed she was having a problem finding the particular one she desired. When I asked what she had in mind, she responded, "I don't know what I want. I am very particular." That was interesting! The two statements are contradictory and exemplary of indecisive thinking. After about *twenty-five minutes*, she picked a package of pens and purchased them. Those cheap pens apparently held more value to her than her time did.

**He who considers too much
will perform little.**
—*Friedrich Schiller*

I admit I am confused when someone wrestles with small and seemingly inconsequential decisions. It seems a senseless waste of energy. If the second or third best choice will still be a good choice for you, you come out a winner. Consider, what is the penalty if you do *not* pick the absolutely very best choice in a relatively insignificant decision?

**In a moment of decision,
the best thing you can do is the right thing to do.
The worst thing you can do is nothing.**
—*Theodore Roosevelt*

I compare moments of indecision to being in a drag race. Your wheels spin madly while your forward progress remains almost motionless. Since indecisive thinking needlessly zaps your energy, indecision potentially causes more harm to you than a wrong decision does.

Rise above contention and agony over small decisions and save that energy for things that matter more.

However, while taking the larger view of life, you should recognize that the *totality* of what you think about and which activities you involve yourself with in the majority of your little moments do themselves become an element of your big picture.

Do It Now

Procrastination results from a decision made by you to do nothing. Your decision may be a passive, non-energized choice, but your thought causes your delay of action.

Procrastination is the thief of time.[2]

At some time, we have all said, "I don't have time." However, we are all allotted the same 168 hours each and every week. If *anyone* finds the time to do some particular thing, then *you* possess the time as well. More appropriately, what you could say is, "I choose other priorities for now."

By establishing the habit of doing things "now" rather than putting off tasks until later, you save time. Of course, you cannot actually "save" time; you merely use your 168-hour allotment of time more to your advantage.

When you choose to put off decisions and activities, more tend to appear and accumulate. Because you feel behind already, many new obligations merely get added to your "to do" list. As the delayed obligations begin piling up, your list grows.

It is generally rewarding for you to tend to matters right away.

The Burdens We Accumulate

Excessive accumulation of possessions is a burden to "collectors of stuff." This unseemly habit is caused by three different types of diseased thinking; indecision ("I can't decide what to do with this"), lazy procrastination ("I will throw it later"), or the fear of losing ("If I throw it away, I might wish for it later").

> **Beware of covetousness,**
> **which is a malady, diseaseful...**
> —*Ptah-hotep*

You first take control of your possessions. Then, without occasional inventory reduction, your material belongings begin to control your existence and become a burden, rather than a benefit, for you. Some people simply bond with their physical possessions. Rather than the person owning physical possessions, the possessions gain control over *the person*—the person's activity and vitality. Excessive possessions clutter your existence, and hinder your capacity for happiness.

**Not the owner of many possessions
will you be right to call happy...**
—Horace (65-8 B.C.)

When you don't keep your stockpiles of worldly possessions in order, your possessions can become exhausting to your spirit, causing you lack of drive and creativity. You experience a constant nagging feeling that something really should be done about this burden of accumulated excess.

Out of clutter, find simplicity.
—Albert Einstein

If you're like most people, feeling your physical house is in order gives your *internal* spirit a boost.

Excesses, by definition, are always bad.
KISS – Keep It Simple, Stupid.

**Our life is frittered away by detail...
simplify, simplify.**
—Henry David Thoreau

Happiness is Not for Sale

People often look outside themselves to obtain happiness. They look to a family member, a friend, or sometimes even to a stranger for gratification. Or rather than petition their own mind for a new way of thinking, they deceive themselves by going out and purchasing a worldly possession in hopes of producing internal joy. In very short order, they find themselves no happier for the purchase.

> **Change your thoughts
> and you change your world.**
> —*Rev. Norman Vincent Peale*

Happiness is produced through your own thought in your own mind and cannot be acquired through any other means.

Creating Value

Money spent on acquiring something does not automatically give value to the acquisition. Real value, whether in a tangible thing or merely in thought, comes through your personal effort and your bond of *emotional* attachment.

> **Only a fool thinks price and value are the same.**
> —*Antonio Machado*

Consider a few points of illustration. Most people love their own child or grandchild more than they love other people, no matter how great or not-so-great the child may be. Or, which holds more meaning—a purchased figurine or the one that Grandpa lovingly hand-whittled special for you? And, it can sometimes be a very tough decision when considering a move to a newer house and out of the home you've lived in, worked on, and owned for the last thirty-five or forty years. There is a value of personal equity for you in each of those things that money cannot buy.

To create greater value for yourself, be willing to expend some effort toward your affection, your desire, or your goal.

> **Try not to become a man of success,**
> **rather become a man of value.**
>
> *—Albert Einstein*

It's Your Hang-up, You Own It

We all find little things in other people that cause irritation for us. Someone you care for may do atrocious things like squeeze the toothpaste tube wrong, load the dishwasher incorrectly, or slouch as they sit. When you are around people a lot, their way of doing things the "wrong" way can become very irritating for you.

You know how to do things in a certain way, and that, of course, is the "right" way. You have logical explanations as to why your way is the right way.

Those little things are *your* hang-ups. They are your possessions. Everyone has her own set of hang-ups. However, you can actually gain control over your hang-ups by letting them go.

Here again, by stepping back and grasping the larger view, you see the relative insignificance in these situations. In order to overcome your small hang-ups, if you regard two maxims noted earlier—*fight only the fight worth fighting* and *view life in the big picture*—you find it easier to place these little irritations in their proper perspective. Then, you just may find it easier to accept your roommate's squeezing the toothpaste in a way other than the way you do.

Loosen up! Gain a new freedom; empower yourself.

Avoid Extremes

Extremes should be avoided. This is a broad, but predominately useful, maxim. There are obvious exceptions, but adopting this as a general rule will serve you well.

Here are some examples to consider. Extremely boring or extremely wild and crazy friends may be negative influences for you in your quest for living the robust life. Both extremely safe and extremely risky investments are generally best avoided as neither is likely to be good for your financial well-being. Extreme diets are not likely to be very satisfying or healthy for you. Being a wasteful spender or an excessive tightwad both prove to be destructive financial management styles that are detrimental to your quest for long-term happiness.

Worry, Fear, and Doubt

There are plenty of other not-so-healthy habits that will gladly nestle into your mindset if you decide to pick the "let happenstance choose for me" method of forming habits.

What is more physically and emotionally draining than worry? Worry is created in your own mind by your own direct order.

Again, developing the habit, mentioned earlier, of viewing life in the big scheme is a beneficial approach to preventing worry. Through worry, you actually plant in your mind the seed of the very situation you wish to avoid. If you want to avoid it, don't go there!

If you permit worry to linger, your mind soon accepts doubt as well. You begin to experience doubt about your own positive possibilities and capabilities.

Fear is an interesting disease because there are good fears (which are actually *not* disease) and there are bad fears. Good fears are essential for your health, while bad fears will, at the very least, make your life less rewarding.

You were born with two natural fears: the fear of falling and fear of loud noises. They are good and useful fears that come to you instinctively. Instinctive fears help you to survive life itself.

However, as you live, you learn to adopt new fears for yourself. Learned fears are generally, but not always, unhealthy for you. They can hold you back and make your life less enjoyable.

We have nothing to fear but fear itself.
—*Franklin Delano Roosevelt*

If your Creator intended for you to be fearful of spiders, mice, and snakes, he likely would have made them part of your instinctive fears. Likewise, if a fear of failure were a beneficial thing for you, he would have built *fear of failure* right into your original programming for survival as well.

**The greatest mistake you can make in life
is to be continually fearing
that you will make one.[3]**

Fear, doubt, and worry will gladly harbor in your mind when allowed. Their existence plays in your mind as a practice rehearsal for your future. Fear, doubt, and worry often hold people back from trying potentially profitable endeavors. Any of the three (fear, doubt, or worry) is quite adept at destroying great possibilities for you. When you allow any, or all three, to flourish in your mind, you destroy your Divinely furnished-at-birth potential for living a fulfilling life.

For your own sake, whenever any of these diseases attempts to gain entry into your mind, check it at the door and replace it with positive possibilities.

It Takes Courage

You can turn negative fear into a mere blip in the road and drive right over it. You can minimize fear by diverting your attention *away* from the fear itself and re-directing your focus *toward your desire*. Your intention or desire can become of greater prominence in your mind than the fear itself.

> **Courage is not the absence of fear, but rather the judgment that something is more important than fear.**
>
> —*Ambrose Redmoon*

The presence of fear is still undeniable. You will not be able to totally destroy fear but you can learn to over-power and *control* your fear.

Later, in chapter eleven, you will discover more detailed instruction on disciplines to assist you in over-powering your fears.

Mind-Body Health Relationships

The health of your thinking will affect your physical health as well. In a way, your body can be considered an appendage of your mind. Your mind has control over the functioning of the body, such as the rhythmic pumping of your heart, your lungs' inhalation and exhalation, digestion of food through your alimentary system, etc.

What you choose to *think* will have a noticeable effect on how well your body performs its physical functions. You can quite literally fear, or worry, yourself sick. The quality of your thought is every bit as influential to your *physical* health as is the type and quality of food that enters the body through your alimentary system. The physical and mental inter-relationship also works in the reverse: a physical ailment can have an effect on the way you think.

How you choose to dress and groom, what habits you take ownership of, your choice of activity and moral conduct, and what profession you choose also hold influence on what you think. More importantly, they hold influence on what you think *of yourself*. If you want to feel "up," dress up. If you want to improve your morals, raise your standard. Your self-image will improve.

Cause and Effect

For every thought you choose to entertain, there is a consequence. For every action you take, there is a consequence. This is referred to as cause and effect. It is a reality of this world you are forced to deal with. You cannot escape it.

Cause is a person or thing that makes something happen. Effect is the something that happens as a result of the cause. Cause directed by you is of vital importance to your happiness. What you think and say and what actions you perform (cause) directly correlate to your degree of happiness and fulfillment (effect).

A simplified example: there is a bucket full of water that you would like emptied. There are several possible actions that might accomplish that purpose.

1. You can dump the water out yourself. This action may be self-satisfying for you, or if you have some affliction, could, instead, cause distress for you.

2. You can ask someone else to dump the water out. The person may gladly help you out, or grudgingly do so. Or the person may completely ignore your request. They may become defiant, and may or may not empty the bucket.

3. You can *demand* that someone else dump the water out. The same possibilities exist as in number two. However, the likelihood of the person cheerfully helping you will be lessened.

4. You may do nothing, realizing that Nature will evaporate the water for you. This would require no effort on anyone's part. However, this choice will take much longer to accomplish and may not satisfy the reason you wanted the bucket emptied in the first place.

Each of these options could effectively empty the bucket, as you desire. However, each could produce varying effects. The level of satisfaction you receive in your endeavor to have the bucket emptied will depend on which cause you pick and the manner in which you express it. In other words, your input (cause) will influence the end result and the degree of satisfaction you derive from it (effect).

Cause always results in effect. Likewise, effect always results from cause. For every thought you think and for every action you take (causes), know there are effects that result.

Happiness Comes from Within

You are responsible for your own happiness. Fate and circumstances have nothing to do with your sense of personal fulfillment. Your own thought, and *only* your thought, determines your happiness.

If you choose prudent thoughts and actions, you can generally determine with relative confidence what the effects will be. Of course, some things happen to you every day that simply are beyond your control. Since that is the case, you will be forced to make choices on how to react to what happens around you. But again, your thought alone, and not the circumstance itself, determines your degree of happiness.

A person may lose an arm and ultimately become a bigger person because of that fate. Another might be the recipient of a big lottery drawing and become lesser for it because of the choices she makes in handling her winnings.

Good thoughts and good actions generally stimulate good results. Good cause, good effect. Seek thought and action to cause that which you desire.

You are not happy because you are well.
You are well because you are happy.
You are not depressed because trouble has come to you,
but trouble has come because you are depressed.
You can change your thoughts and feelings,
and then the outer things will come to correspond,
and indeed there is no other way of working.

—Emmet Fox

Adversity Does Not Mean Hardship

Difficulties lie directly on your path toward growth and personal development. Do not drive around them.

Your disappointments and failures give you cause to reflect on ways to improve. Typically you expend more effort reflecting on the course of your failures than your successes. A reflective focus searching for improvement is less likely to surface when things are going smoothly for you. New perspectives, new ideas that produce positive results often come as a result of problem solving. You experience greater opportunity for growth when facing challenge. When you encounter no problems, you are likely to experience little self-growth.

A smooth sea never made a skilled mariner.

—English proverb

The more obstacles and hardships you overcome in working toward a goal, the more rewarding your ultimate conquest will feel.

When I was a youngster, I had a small business of raising geese.

Whenever the day arrived for a hatch of new babies, I always felt concern for the little goslings as it seemed they had to struggle so hard in making their way out of the egg shell and into the new world. I usually assisted them with their struggles by pulling the shell apart and helping them out.

As I recall, I experienced a lot of disappointing new hatches. There were many new little goslings that were sprawl-legged, with their legs sticking out to each side. Many of the newly hatched baby goslings did not survive due to weakness.

Unfortunately, it was not until I was an adult that I learned a pertinent lesson. In my desire to be kind to my little gosling friends, I instead weakened them. By helping them to avoid the struggle provided by Nature, I unwittingly crippled them. They came into this world unprepared for what lay ahead.

Grappling with difficulties holds the same benefit for humanity.

As much as you probably do not appreciate them at the time, challenges are good for you as well. Struggles and deliberate reflection are beneficial and necessary for intellectual growth. Indeed, without the challenges that stimulate growth, this world would not be worth spending your time in.

Don't wish it were easier;
wish you were better.
Don't wish for less problems;
wish for more skills.
Don't wish for less challenges;
wish for more wisdom.[4]

All growth comes from breaking a previous barrier. Without pushing to the limit, and beyond, your abilities never change. We are born as little babies with an innate desire to push for new growth. Ideally, that push for new-ness and developmental growth will persist for you until your departure from this earthly life.

When you truly understand the advantage your hard-ships and challenges offer, you will thank your Creator for providing you with these opportunities. You will grow, you will live, as Henry David Thoreau put it, "with a license of a higher order of beings."

All the adversity I've had in my life,
all my troubles and obstacles,
have strengthened me...
You may not realize it when it happens,
but a kick in the teeth may be the best thing
in the world for you.
—Walt Disney

Some people are blessed (or cursed, depending on your viewpoint) with strikingly attractive physical features. If that is your condition, it becomes an art to use that physical characteristic to your advantage, rather than become vain and thereby turn your physical beauty into ill fortune. It is not every mind, or person, who is of character able to handle the gift of physical beauty with dignity and grace. Many choose to waste their gift of physical attractiveness as a flamboyant decoration used only in seeking pleasure for themselves in a worldly way.

It seems someone with a physical appearance that is considered unattractive to the rest of humanity has a comparative disadvantage. However, to cope in this somewhat discordant world, the mind of a less attractive person must compensate for attaining that which is generally more readily offered to someone with natural physical beauty. The mind of a less attractive person, being unburdened with the distractions that normally accompany someone of physical beauty, often gains advantage by developing a superior mindset.

Crisis Means Opportunity

When you experience problems in your life, it can be an awful feeling. When you are in crisis, at your very lowest point and feeling overwhelmed by the trial of hardship, you can benefit by recognizing that things can *only* get better.

The Japanese symbol for the word *crisis* appropriately consists of a combination of symbols for two other words: *danger* and *opportunity*. Each of those words is appropriate in describing what crisis presents to you.

Since crisis occurs at or near the worst point, it is that point at which you begin to focus on opportunity for yourself rather than the chaos and discord around you.

Your fears and worry hold only the power you give them. Rather than focusing on where you have come from or what you once had, a crisis presents opportunity to concentrate on *growth*.

> **Keep your mind on the objective,**
> **not the obstacle.**
> —*William Randolph Hearst*

The low point of crisis is indeed a time of opportunity, however disguised it appears at the time.

Ah, But We Do Exaggerate

In the days of my youth, I listened on the radio to an interview of a sports star. Today, his name escapes me but the interviewee was a professional baseball pitcher and was also the son of a professional pitcher. When asked, he passed along the best advice his father ever gave him. Father said to son, "Always remember, you are never as good or as bad as you think you are." That was sage advice.

> **We do not deal much in facts**
> **when we are contemplating ourselves.**
> —*Mark Twain*

Your ego has a natural series of checks and balances to it. When things go extremely in the direction you desire, you may tend to begin thinking yourself more invincible than you truly are. When you begin feeling a bit of arrogant superiority, Nature provides a slamming correction to your ego, forcing your thinking back closer to reality. On the other hand, when you make a series of mistakes and begin to feel a sense of inadequacy, Nature brings your senses back closer to reality by providing you with a portrayal of the greatness you have within.

Most likely, you generally think your personal situation is bigger than it actually is. Whether good or bad, much of your own exaggerated *self*-account will go relatively unnoticed by others.

To illustrate the point, try to recall the names of some recent year's Olympic champions, or last year's Cy Young Award winner, or five CEO picks that large businesses recently selected as their choices for overall leader of the company. All these people certainly earned the right to be proud of their remarkable accomplishments. The respective accomplishments of each likely loom large in their *own* reflective view. However, at the same time, it is likely you were not able to recall the names of very many of those people.

Truth and Understanding

You are able to grow on the intellectual level freely and unencumbered when two conditions exist in your mind.

First, you need to see things as they *actually* exist, rather than merely as "truths" that you *desire* to filter into your hard drive. The reality that exists, whether it be pleasing, or ugly and unpalatable, is called truth.

After acknowledging what the real truth is, if you are able to comprehend also the how and the why of the truth's presence, you acquire understanding. Once you attain understanding of how or why a condition exists, you can exercise control over that condition.

> **Nothing in life is to be feared.**
> **It is only to be understood.**
> —*Marie Curie*

A wise guru once sat on a mountaintop. When approached for the secret in acquiring wisdom, she replied, "You want to become wise? Seek truth and understanding. First, seek truth that is *actual* truth; then, seek to understand *why* that truth is."

> **We don't receive wisdom;**
> **we must discover it for ourselves**
> **after a journey that no one**
> **can take for us or spare us.**
> —*Marcel Proust*

Cultivation of Moral Character

Your true character can be determined by what you choose to do and how you choose to act when you think no one else will observe, or by how you treat others who can return neither retaliation nor recompense to you. In other words, your character is revealed when you do totally and completely what you choose according to a standard answerable *only* to yourself. In such situations, there are no expectations of peers to deal with, and there is no external sense of shame or honor to regard. Your thought or your act at such times is what exists within you; it is a display of your true character.

Development of ethical character requires *self*-discipline. No parent, supervisor, or peer can create a high and noble character on your behalf. Others can provide plenty of positive examples and display an expectation of conscientious behavior from you, but your own character can be built only by you, and you alone.

Every man stamps value on himself…
man is made great or small by his own will.
—*J.C.F. von Schiller*

When you choose to cheat or deceive, believing you have little or no chance of being found out, you are deceiving yourself. There is a monumental cost in trying to keep your deceptive guise secret. While potential discovery by others would cause humiliation or embarrassment for you, of more serious consequence is what happens within your own mind. When you cheat, you *are* found out, every time, by the person who is most influential to your happiness— you. When you cheat, you devalue your own character.

Considering each thought you think tends to spread or move toward *your next thought*, you indeed do much damage by lowering your standard simply because it hurts no one else.

There is only one real failure
in life that is possible,
and that is not to be true
to the best one knows.
—*John Farrar*

By lowering your own standard, thereby hurting yourself, realize you *do* hurt others also. You do not live in a vacuum all by yourself. Your values rub off and assign themselves to those you associate with. We all feed off each other.

Your Comfort Zone

You feel safe and secure with familiar possessions, with familiar people, and in familiar surroundings. The relative predictability of each provides a sense of comfort in your life.

That sense of comfort and security is a bit like what a lion that has spent his whole life in a cage feels. The cage offers the lion that same peaceful serenity and predictability. His cage has become his comfort zone.

But the unpredictability, the unplanned occasion, the unknown that may occur is what makes life so rich in possibilities. Predictability offers you monotony. There is no thrill in staying in the cage or in your own comfort zone.

Take a step outside your comfort zone. Then two. Then a third. Keep going!

Then, in the future, when you may feel a bit insecure and desire to step back for a moment into your cage that offers comfort, you will find the cage itself has expanded for you. Your comfort zone has enlarged.

As your comfort zone grows through encompassing more and greater experiences, *you* are able to expand further and further as you step outside the previous zone. The arena of new possibilities for you increases.

**Only in growth, reform, and change,
paradoxically enough,
is true security to be found.**
—*Anne Morrow Lindbergh*

My daughter is an excellent example of one willing to expand her comfort zone for the mere offer of thrill and new experience.

Upon attaining her degree in education, she sought her first teaching job in a foreign country. That in itself, at least for me, would be getting out of one's comfort zone. She spent her first year in South Korea tutoring children in English as a second language.

At the end of the school year, she considered the security of simply retaining the same teaching position for a second year. However, she was offered, and accepted, the step up to teaching adult tutors and teachers how to improve their English teaching skills.

The third year, she was considering yet another change. She had been offered a position as instructor at the college level.

In letting her parents know what she was considering, she felt, as she had a year earlier, it would be very easy to simply settle back and do what she had become accustomed to in her present position. That is, the same job, same school, same curriculum, with a new group of students.

Then she declared, "But that isn't what I'm looking for. I want my job to be more challenging than that."

**All growth...
is the result of risk-taking.**
—Jude Wanniski

I don't think she gave the idea of a repeat performance another thought. She accepted the new challenge. Her comfort zone just kept expanding bigger and bigger, each step granting her ever more opportunity.

She inspires me.

Listening Effectively

By learning to be a good listener, you acquire a very beneficial skill—a skill that relatively few people choose to claim as their own.

In conversation, many people employ the detrimental habit of considering what their *own* response is going to be, even as the other person is speaking. If you find yourself restlessly waiting to speak while you half-heartedly listen, you are not fully hearing the message being presented. And when the speaker is aware you cannot wait to have your say, she surmises your feelings toward her—what *you* have to say is more important than what *she* is saying.

One of the most effective ways to both show respect and, at the same time, earn respect, is to be an attentive listener.

Another significant benefit to becoming a more proficient listener is you naturally acquire greater knowledge.

All the habits you adopt, whether haphazardly or by choice, have a profound effect on who you are and who you will become in the future. Your habits are a significant part of you. It is wise and beneficial to recognize that you always have a choice in which habits you take ownership of.

CHAPTER 5

OPTIMISM

It is advantageous for a person to hold an open and optimistic mindfulness.

People find more pleasure in fellowship with an optimistic person than a pessimistic person. They generally respond more favorably to someone who displays a healthy and buoyant optimism. Furthermore, when a person is able to remain upbeat and spirited through optimism, it becomes more difficult for an outside influence to diminish that person's energy.

Pessimists argue that if they set themselves up to expect the worst, they will never be disappointed with the outcome. The rationale in that mentality may sound great in theory. The delusion in that thinking, however, is your mind does not work in that fashion.

Your mind has an amazing drive to work toward and acquire that which you think about. You might want to re-read that sentence until it becomes deeply ingrained in your subconscious mind as one your profound truths. Once you accept that truth, you begin to realize you can never again afford to think a negative thought. The dominion in your mind of that truth will benefit you more than the presence of any other secular thought.

When I was in my twenties and not of such an optimistic nature as I am today, I worked a construction job,
which I did not find very pleasurable. I was looking for
a change. After researching different options, I decided I
wanted to become a real estate salesperson. When I told
one of my friends on the construction job that I was going
to make the change, his thought was, "Gosh, Greg, you
have to be an optimist for that job."

My response was, "I'm not an optimist or a pessimist.
I'm a realist!"

Moving forward on my life's timeline eighteen or
nineteen years, my brother and I were sharing leisurely
conversation and the subject of attitudes and optimism
and pessimism came up. I made a comment extolling the
virtue and advantage of acquiring an optimistic nature.

His exact quote was, "I'm not an optimist or a pessimist. I'm a realist!" It was *déjà vu.*

My reply, "This world is full of optimists and pessimists, and I believe they are *all* realists." Whether you
choose to accept the positive or the negative outlook, what
you believe will quite likely determine your own reality.
Your thoughts and your attitude create your reality.

> **A pessimist sees the difficulty
> in every opportunity;
> an optimist sees the opportunity
> in every difficulty.**
> —*Winston Churchill*

Again, your mind has an amazing ability to work toward
and acquire that which you think about. Your mind cannot

afford to be of pessimistic nature. It is simply too costly to your personal well being and health. There is nothing positive to be gained through a negative expectation. Nothing. You will definitely *not* gain the absence of disappointment by adopting a negative personality. On the contrary.

Those who focus on negative possibilities are not capable of *earning* positive possibilities. Negative thinkers can only *hope* that Lady Luck will find favor and grant an unexpected positive outcome. Should that occur, even then, a negative person will not be capable of accepting the windfall unless she is able to recondition her mind into a state able to accept the positive result.

The subconscious mind's desire to achieve what is fixated within is related to why prayers of request, when petitioned with a sense of expectancy, often yield positive results. People praying to their Divine Benefactor with the belief that their request *will* be fulfilled additionally benefit from their own subconscious mind's inclination to work toward *its* expectation.

The Communication Link to Your Creator

Your subconscious mind is the direct link your Creator uses to communicate with you.

Your subconscious mind is your very essence. Everything stored within your subconscious mind, whether good or bad, helpful or harmful, happy or sad, memories that can be brought to the conscious surface or memories that cannot be willfully brought up, are all part of your essence. Your subconscious mind is filled with so many memories and so much stored data that *you* do not even totally know yourself.

But your Creator does. He knows who you are and directs his creative thoughts to the real you, that is, your subconscious mind. With your Creator's presence there, is it any wonder that your subconscious mind is capable of doing virtually anything you can conceive?

> **Whatever the mind of man can conceive and believe, it can achieve.**
> —*Napoleon Hill*

Noble thoughts come from fully utilizing this interactive link with your Creator. Unsound thought is derived by ignoring this powerful alliance and trying to "go it alone."

Your Brain Filter

You develop biases based on what information you take into your mind. As any bit of new information is presented to you, your mind instantly decides whether this bit of information is of significant value, some value, or of no value at all to you. Every piece of data presented for your consideration is instantly catalogued according to its determined significance. The more significance, the greater the prominence within the brain's filing system. Things your mind determines to be of no significance may not register at all.

Each of us has created a filter for ourselves in deciding what is acceptable food for our mind and what is not.

That is necessary simply because there is so much conflicting input being thrown at you. Without the filter, your mind would accept everything it is subjected to. Your beliefs would, at times, be jumping from one extreme to the opposite extreme, one second to the next. The brain filter, when properly maintained and unclogged, is both a necessary and good thing.

At the same time, the brain filter can also become a hindrance for you. With all the data being presented to your brain for consideration, it is easy to become effortlessly comfortable and biased in your thinking. You begin to hear what you *want* to hear, and see what you *want* to see.

**We do not err because truth is difficult to see...
we err because this is more comfortable.**

—*Alexander Solzhenitsyn*

Your Ever-changing State of Limbo

On a conscious level you direct your thoughts to whatever you choose. Your subconscious mind takes in and accepts as "truth" whatever you *choose* to feed it. Usually this takes place without your conscious awareness that change is occurring within.

The character of your mind is in a constant state of limbo. That means, at every moment you are developing a new self.

You possess the ability to point the direction toward which your internal change will go—always. Not only the ability, but, because of the way you are wired, your self-direction becomes inescapable. You *must* choose because your mind and your own thought have complete authority over your direction. And you cannot escape your own mind or your own thought; you can only direct it.

Anytime some action over which you have no control happens to you, you necessarily choose what to accept out of the occurrence and what your reaction is going to be. Your subconscious mind accepts as "truth," or discards as rubbish, whatever you choose.

Many people ultimately end up requiring psychiatric therapy and/or hypnosis in order to "manually reprogram" a particularly hurtful or harmful idea they allowed into their subconscious mind.

Feed yourself (your mind, that is) carefully.

There were twin brothers who grew up in a family with a father who was severely alcoholic. The father had little time for the boys as his habit of excessive drinking took all priority.

When the boys grew up to become adults, one of the boys became a shiftless derelict drunk himself. When forced into therapeutic treatment for his debilitating condition, his explanation was, "When you look at my father, how could anyone expect *me* to be any different?"

His brother chose quite a different lifestyle. He owned his own business and devoted much time to his community. He became a very respected man and a stellar example for his family. When asked, in consideration of his father's influence in his childhood, how he had turned out so different from his father and so distinguished, his response was, "How could anyone *expect* me to be the same as he was?"

> **There is always reason in the man for his good or bad fortune.**
> —*Ralph Waldo Emerson*

Each brother chose a series of habits and a thought process to adopt for himself. When contemplating his lifestyle, each was able to justify being the person he became. Their responses revealed some of their adopted "truths."

Count on Luck

Luck involves the element of chance. It can be good for you or it can bad for you. We are all subject to the whims of luck; luck will not be denied. However, Lady Luck cannot be relied on to be around at all times, through thick and thin. She is fickle, and only she decides when to announce her presence.

The only sure thing about luck is that it will change.
—*Brett Hart*

Luck has a mystical quality; luck seems to have little rhyme or reason to its time of appearance. However, when luck does reveal its presence, regardless of whether it is good or bad luck, there seems to be a pattern of ebb and flow. At times, you can be bombarded with one unlucky misfortune after another, while, other times, no matter how unqualified or incompetent your own performance, Lady Luck repeatedly smiles upon you with no coerced inducement on your part.

Those who expect to gain nothing from Lady Luck will miss much of what is being offered to them. Be attentive and prepared for her.

> **I will prepare, and someday
> my chance will come.**
> —*Abraham Lincoln*

The astute person will be prepared to cut losses quickly when Lady Luck is not being fortuitous. Likewise, the wise and skillful person will be ready for Lady Luck to spread her good fortune and to capitalize on opportunity. Wise people use good luck to their advantage.

Your Thoughts are Contagious

Whether you express your thoughts by verbalization or through body language and demeanor, others around you feel your influence. What you think, your very being, helps shape the minds around you.

> **We rise to each other's expectations,
> or we fall to them.**
> —*Lou Tice*

Others around you adopt your attitude, at least to some degree. Whether you are lethargic or enthusiastic and vivacious, a part of your disposition is rubbing off on someone.

Most people agree, optimists are just fun company to be around. Help make the world a happier place. Make it your conscious choice to be optimistic and enthusiastic.

CHAPTER 6

MARRIAGE AND PARENTING

Even though marriage and parenting seem to go hand-in-hand, they are two very different things. In order to be beneficial and fulfilling to all parties involved, each of these responsibilities requires very different skills.

Marriage

The partner you pick as your mate for life will have a profound effect on your future. This may be true even if you later decide to terminate the marriage. If children are involved, it becomes virtually impossible to terminate the relationship altogether.

When young lovers marry, they have little clue what the future of their relationship holds. They may dream of having their own home someday and a happy family together. But young lovers pretty much take their new spouse for better or for worse, blinded by affection and an ambiguous dream.

Later they learn that love and the matrimonial relationship are not something they can simply take for granted.

Things change. People change. Your love for each other changes, just as change affects *any* living entity. And, realize, your relationship with your spouse *is* a living entity. Your marital relationship evolves based on the development of its two ever-changing partners. In order for the marriage to survive "till death do you part," as with anything that is alive, your relationship needs constant care and feeding. Nurturing and affection, attentive regard, and respect for each other are basic sustenance for a thriving marriage.

The person you married at twenty-three is not the person that you will be married to at seventy-three. Furthermore, you will not be the same person your spouse married as a youngster. That is a good thing since both you and your spouse might get tired of being married to someone that acts like a twenty-three-year-old! Over time, that starry-eyed love present in younger days reaches a different level of maturity. You begin to realize love does not simply continue just because you married each other.

Be wary of assuming your married status should offer you a sense of security. That commitment and togetherness merely offers greater opportunity for both of you to grow ever stronger and closer in your relationship. As is required in courtship, in order for your *marital* relationship to flourish, you need to continue feeling sensitivity toward your mate's wants and needs. In a robust and fulfilling marital relationship, the excitement and joy of *dating* your mate continues even after you "tie the knot."

There is no greater excitement than to support an intellectual wife and have her support you.
—*Millicent Carey McIntosh*

It Takes Commitment

Does a marriage really turn two individuals into one couple? Yes, that union does create a whole new entity. Yet, for the marriage to thrive, each spouse needs to respect the individuality of his or her mate.

(referring to marriage)
**To keep the fire burning brightly,
there's one easy rule:
keep the two logs together,
near enough to keep each other warm and
far enough apart for breathing room.**
—*Marnie Reed Crowell (paraphrased)*

It is in the best interest of your union and, likewise, for each of you as individuals to continually bring out the best in both your partner and yourself. Your joined relationship will be only as rewarding as each of you makes it. By assisting your spouse in building his or her self-esteem, you cannot help but add to your own sense of worth in the process. If yours is a marriage involving commitment and real love for each other, your partner's personal development and growth will become as important to you as your own.

**It is mind, not body,
that makes marriage last.**
—*Publilius Syrus, 1ˢᵗ century B.C.*

If you give, without condition, more than your fair share to your marriage, and your partner reciprocates with more than his or her fair share, you will find a respect and joy that can last until death. Long and healthy marriages occur as a result of development of mutual empathy and commitment to one another.

Commitment requires more than passivity. Assuming and maintaining a relationship of commitment continually requires your conscious thought and effort.

> **A successful marriage requires
> falling in love many times,
> always with the same person.**
> —*Mignon McLaughlin*

Divorce

The relationship of a couple that is strongly committed to one another does not collapse.

Anyone involved in a meaningful marriage will, at times, be involved in disagreement with their spouse. If you care, you will sometimes fight. *Because* you care is the very reason a fight occurs in the first place. Be thankful for that much.

However, with petty and relatively insignificant fighting, it is always okay to simply know you are right without forcing your opinion down your spouse's throat. It is even prudent to acquiesce to your partner sometimes, even when you just know he or she is totally off base and you are the genius on this one.

Rather than doing any major damage, disagreements can be kept relatively inconsequential if the parties choose to keep them so.

When someone chooses the action of divorcing a spouse, oftentimes, they are simply trading one set of problems for a new set of problems. When considering dissolution, rather than renouncing the marriage itself, the internal thinking of the two partners may simply be in need of filter cleaning. The rationalization in your mind that creates the desire to discard your partner and the relationship may be in need of alteration. Likely, *both* your and your spouse's way of looking at the situation needs some adjustment.

If, however, your partnership truly is detrimental to your health, either physically or mentally, and there appears to be no reasonable chance for rectification, you gain nothing by toughing it out. You deserve all the bliss life has to offer and tying yourself to an impossibly difficult condition takes that opportunity away from you.

But, always bear in mind, salvaging and refurbishing your marriage may be easier *and* more rewarding than divorce. Before choosing to bail on your marital relationship, make an honest effort to re-discover the love you once were capable of. If devotion and respect were possible earlier, they may *still* be quite possible for both of you. You have a vested interest in this partner and in this relationship. More times than not, if each of you invests new effort toward rekindling your bond and attraction for one another, you can inspire renewed joy in your marriage.

Foundation First, Fireplace Later

A sound long-term relationship requires a strong base, a solid foundation.

Some couples choose early in their relationship to indulge in the act of sex. No commitment of any kind—just sex for the pleasure of sensual gratification. Then they try to build a relationship off that superficial adventure. With an indiscriminately promiscuous initiation, the chance of developing a meaningful relationship backed by respect and mutual trust is suspect.

Building a relationship can be compared to building a physical structure. No experienced builder would build the fireplace first, then the room around it, then the house, and finally try to add the foundation to make the whole structure solid. That would be extremely difficult at best.

Meaningful long-term relationships require a base of trust and respect for each other. A frivolous roll in the hay early in a relationship holds potential to undermine your feelings of trust or respect for one another. Your behavior indicates your personal standard of moral character.

Start with the base, build on that, and let a heartfelt and meaningful intimacy become the fireplace that is added later.

Jealousy vs. Empowerment

When someone in a human relationship consents to feeling jealousy, all parties involved lose. Jealousy and envy occur when someone of fragile character feels a need to equalize his or her position by suppressing the other party's autonomy and self-expression. A vulnerability to jealousy diminishes the bonds of a relationship, and, if unchecked, will likely eventually destroy the relationship.

That is true of *any* relationship involving humans. It is true of marriage, a parent-child relationship, teacher and student, or boss and employee.

The opposite of yielding to jealousy is the act of empowering. Rather than using energy trying to suppress another party, instead bestow honor on her. Point out her merits. You empower another person by building up her feeling of worth.

Spouses often point out each other's deficiencies. Instead, we should be each other's motivator.

—Gladys Knight

By assisting someone in discovering her own competence, you accomplish more than simply empowering the other person. Your act provides an element of distinction for the other person *and yourself.* Certainly the recipient of a compliment appreciates the prestige endowed upon her; however, the donor of goodwill often benefits to an even greater dimension.

When you do good deeds for someone, it naturally makes you feel good yourself. By building up others, you strengthen your own character and feeling of worth. The other party gains, you gain; everyone wins.

Parenting

When you decide to take on parenthood, you accept the most important responsibility in this world. As an infant, your child is 100 percent dependent on others for comfort, nurturing, and growth. Eighteen years later, she is ready to conquer the world! It takes an incredible variety of skills to get your child from point A to point B.

Although your child is born with some inherent physical and intellectual features, the greatest factor in your young child's mental character comes through the day-to-day influence of parents, siblings, and other prominent individuals. The preparation, education, and training of your child holds great significance that will influence her for the rest of her life.

> **Life affords no greater responsibility,
> no greater privilege,
> than the raising of the next generation.**
> —*C. Everett Koop, M.D.*

All parents, from time to time, find themselves feeling a bit overwhelmed by the enormity of responsibility and effort that comes with child rearing. At such times, you can easily lose sight of the big picture, which, in turn, can cause needless anxiety.

In times of trouble, it is helpful to remember there are plenty of parents (who may make good mentors, by the way) who have already experienced a very similar incident to what you are going through. In fact, in our modern age of high technology and intelligence, children have not changed to any significant degree from children of centuries past.

An inscription found on a *six-thousand-year-old* Egyptian tomb reads, "We are in a decaying age. Young people no longer respect their parents. They are rude and impatient. They inhabit taverns and have no self-control." Does that sound like anything you have heard in *your own* lifetime?

The trouble you experience in raising your child is likely not as unique and as provoking as it may appear to you, as a parent. Others have been through a very similar scenario before; your child is not so bad.

One of the most effective means of getting to know and earning the respect of your child is to offer your child a significant amount of your time and your full attention. Those two things, and your love, mean more to your child than anything in the world. Make certain your child knows she is loved without reservation and without any strings attached. You love her no matter what.

Of equal importance is to show your child she comes from, and is a member of, a loving *family*. Show her she is the result of a loving relationship. Do not be afraid to show lots of displays of tasteful and appropriate (that is, family rated) affection toward your spouse in front of your child.

Many marriage partners yield their marriage to the status of being on auto-pilot during the child-rearing years. That can be a grave mistake. The marriage itself should not suffer because you have a child. Besides, when your marriage suffers, the child suffers. Even though each of you may have the best intention for the child you both love, when your marriage fails, the effectiveness of your parenting skills become dramatically hampered. Your child deserves the best parenting capabilities you possess. For your child's sake, energize and appreciate your marriage and your marriage partner as fully and vibrantly as you can.

**The most important thing
that a father can do for his children
is to love their mother.**
—*Theodore Hesburgh*

Catch your child doing something good as often as you can. Catch your kid being a good person. Let her know you noticed. Let her know she makes you proud. Not only are her actions good, but she is good.

Conversely, when her actions are not so good, let her know you are not so pleased with the negative activity, but she is still loved. It is not the child who is bad, but rather the activity that is bad.

Is that being hypocritical, when there is good activity to praise the person, and when there is negative activity to criticize the action itself? No, that's good parenting. That is effective parenting.

In conditioning your child's thinking, you merely plant the realization in her subconscious mind that she is a doer of good activities she can be proud of. She is a good person. If you help make the kid *think* she is a good person who does good things, she will become the person she thinks she is.

> **They are able because they think they are able.**
> —*Virgil, poet 70-19 BC*

It is encouraging to a dedicated and loving parent to realize the positive mindset being developed in your child holds potential to stick with her for the rest of her life.

Every loving parent will want to take note that it is far easier to introduce positive programming into your young child than for *her* to try re-programming her subconscious mind as an adult. Parents, you possess awesome power!

A responsibility comes with that power. As extremely influential people in your child's life, you have an obligation not only to her, but to all of Creation, in doing all the good you can in raising your child.

There are limitations, however, in how much influence even a parent has on their child's development. If two "perfect" parents were to exist and were fortunate enough to be married to each other, that condition would *still* not guarantee great and productive offspring. It would merely improve the availability of opportunity for that child's growth.

Each child is unique and will respond to influence in her own fashion.

Discipline

Discipline should not be construed as being a negative thing. Practicing discipline is wise and gainful, whether used in the training of yourself or of someone dependent on you for training.

Children have more need of models than of critics.
—*Carolyn Coats*

Sometimes when children misbehave, as they all do from time to time, it becomes necessary to discipline. There are different forms of disciplinary action, some of which *are* just plain harmful rather than beneficial to your child. But nonetheless, discipline is a tool that is good and useful in rearing children.

> ## We have neglected to discipline our children and called it building self-esteem.
> —*Minister Joe Wright*

Sadly, some parents think they just can't discipline their little child because they love the child sooooo much. These parents seem oblivious to the fact that they actually harm their child by avoiding teaching her skills that will benefit her.

Discipline is a fundamental principle to be utilized in living a rewarding and fruitful life. The need for discipline is as applicable for training a child as it is for an adult exercising self-discipline.

As parents, my wife and I found both time-outs and slow "counts to five" to be very effective parenting tools. However, the impending consequence of further discipline had to be real in order for these to be useful training strategies.

There has to be a consequence when your Little Johnny bullies the scrawny kid on the playground. If you don't induce consequences, Johnny is likely to continue the offensive behavior until someday when someone less loving than his parent *does* take disciplinary action. The disciplinary consequences delivered at that time, by someone other than a parent, will likely be more threatening to Johnny's happiness and well-being. Besides, with time, Johnny's harmful behavioral habits, after years of time, become more difficult to reverse, if Johnny is even able to recognize the need for improvement in his behavior and *then* willing to make the effort.

Every child deserves to learn the rudiments of discipline by parents. Those fundamentals, when properly administered, become the basis for practicing self-discipline later in life.

You should never use *fear of you* as a disciplinary tool in teaching a child. Fear brings behavioral compliance for a short while, but in the long run the use of fear breeds resentment and rebellion.

A peace which depends upon fear is nothing but a suppressed war.
—Henry van Dyke

As a teaching aid, using reward as a motivational tool is more effective than imposing punishment.[5] Gaining a reward lets your child feel appreciated for her positive activity and, naturally, creates a desire to replicate the positive performance.

Correction does much, but encouragement does more.
—Johann Wolfgang von Goethe

Developing your child's respect through nurturing is more effective than trying to force her respect through punishment and fear of punishment. Help your child develop a healthy and loving respect for you as parents.

Encourage Your Child's Individuality

If your child is going to live *her* life and truly be herself, she needs nurturing toward that objective. As your child develops a feeling of self-worth, her own unique character, to some degree, develops naturally. However, at times her individuality will need to be encouraged through skillful and proficient teachers, mentors, and you, as a parent. All of us, children and adults alike, often need an extra push, or encouragement, before we dare plunge into the unknown territory just outside our cage of comfort.

Many parents make the mistake of living their lives through the activities of their child. However, as a parent, realize you can, and should, live your own life and experience your own desires *and*, at the same time, assist your child in discovering *her own* spirit.

> **The teacher who is indeed wise does not bid you to enter the house of his wisdom but rather leads you to the threshold of your mind.**
> —*Kahlil Gibran*

When I was in high school, I thought I would enjoy participating in the sport of wrestling. However, I did not get the opportunity.

In later years, when my own son entered junior high, I strongly encouraged him to try wrestling as a sport. He was not particularly interested, but still I persisted. Ryan did go out for wrestling. However, he found the sport not to his liking and the following year wanted to drop out of the program.

That's when I realized my mistake. I was wrong. I had been trying to live my own fantasy life through my child. It was not so much for *his* benefit that I encouraged Ryan, but more for mine. I wanted to express *my* individuality through my son's activity.

With that realization, I quickly supported his decision.

Peer Pressure

We humans hold innate desire to feel respected and accepted. Because the desire for acceptance is such a powerful force, the most prevalent and controlling fear for most people is a fear of rejection, especially rejection by our peers. That dominating fear results in feeling "peer pressure."

What is peer pressure? Peer pressure is coercion or influence by others that makes you feel you should act in a way you don't really want to, or in a way that wouldn't otherwise be normal for you. Peer pressure can be either a negative or a positive influence, although people generally think of peer pressure in the negative sense.

We often think of peer pressure as being a teen problem. Adolescents, in their fragile state of transition from child to adult, often feel more confusion (as compared to other phases in life), and have a greater need to feel that they "fit in." Because of their feeling of insecurity, adolescents do indeed have a greater tendency to succumb to peer pressure. However, since everyone has peers, we *all* experience the effects of peer pressure.

While attending a social banquet, an adult, after sitting down for the meal, may notice a significant number of other people putting their napkins on their laps. Even though it is not something she normally does before eating a meal, this time, she quietly places her napkin on her lap. By doing so, she submits to social peer pressure.

Trust and Be Trustworthy

Your child is likely to adopt principles and a sense of ethics similar to what you, her parents, embrace. As her parents, you serve as her logical and most readily available mentors. The character of your principles may not be so apparent in her developmental years, but as adults, most of us embody principles and moral character similar to what we observed while growing up.

When going to the movie theater, say the age break for lower ticket prices is eleven and younger. Are you tempted to say your twelve-year-old is actually eleven to save a dollar or two? If you do, you teach your child that lying for money is acceptable behavior.

Do not think twice about it; spend the dollar. It will be a great, *and* low-cost, investment in your child's education. A dollar well spent.

Generally, your children live up to or down to your expectations. Develop a trusting relationship with your children. It empowers both them and you.

> **It is the nature of man to rise to greatness if greatness is expected of him.**
>
> —*John Steinbeck*

My wife and I made a continual point in raising our four children that we trusted them, and would continue to trust them until they proved to us they were *not* to be trusted. They did not disappoint us.

Did that mean they were perfect kids 100 percent of the time? No, of course not. But then, we did not expect perfection either. They made some mistakes and that's OK.

No relationship can be fulfilling without the presence of mutual respect and a sense of trust. By displaying trust in your child, communication lines between child and parent remain relatively open. When a kid feels trusted, she's likely to be trustworthy. And when she's being good and trustworthy, she doesn't need to fudge on the truth.

Children are likely to live up to what you believe of them.
—Lady Bird Johnson

Conversely, show your child she is *not* trusted, and she will likely come through with actions to justify your distrust.

By granting a feeling of trust toward your child and being trustworthy yourself, both child and parent gain liberty to develop their own individuality. Each gains an empowering freedom.

Learning Effective Parenting Skills

Consider the huge responsibility parents hold in raising a child. Parents often feel inundated from all sides when trying to balance a work schedule, household duties and maintenance, a marital relationship, their child's school and other activities, *and* a harmonious family environment. It can be daunting when you further consider the mindset developed in the first years of your child's life sets the tone for the remaining years of her life.

Parenting remains the most important job in the world; yet it is available to anyone able to adopt or give birth to a baby. Having a baby is the *only* requirement to get the position!

Considering the many varied skills required for effective parenting and how early training enormously influences your child's whole life, it is a sad predicament that parenting skills and standards are simply left to chance. The parents you are born to, or have been adopted by, become your primary nurturers, whether or not they are capable.

Other skilled jobs require training. Sometimes employers demand years of higher education before a person will even be given consideration as a candidate for a position of employment. Many work positions necessitate further skills training after the company hires them. Yet, there is no training required for the most-important responsibility of parenting.

Do not simply obtain your parenting skills while going through the process of trial and error. That can be a very costly experience! Although learning effective skills is not required to obtain the position of being a parent, your child's positive development can be more assured by proactively seeking parent training for yourself.

Stay-at-Home Parents

Fifty years ago, a fifty-hour workweek was commonplace. Today, society considers a forty-hour week the norm. Unless, of course, you consider the fact many people feel they simply can't make it on a forty-hour paycheck, so, to make ends meet, they work overtime hours or take on a second job.

As a result, many workers once again spend less time at home with their spouse and children, not unlike the situation decades ago.

However, to make matters worse, now it is commonplace to find *both* parents choosing to work outside the home. "Latchkey kids" routinely arrive home from school to an empty house. There is real tragedy in that! Parents, being primary teachers and mentors, need to *spend time and effort* with their children if they expect to influence their children.

Today, your neighbors have more grand cars than anyone had fifty years ago. Many people own larger, fancier homes with central air-conditioning and heat, and they wear more spiffy clothes, complete with designer labels proudly displayed.

Consider, if that is what is important to the neighbors, maybe you will be better off *not* wanting to keep up with the neighbors. What is of such importance that your child has to do without either parent for a significant part of the day, day after day, week after week?

> I have learned why people
> work so hard to succeed:
> it is because they envy
> the things their neighbors have.
> But it is useless.
> It is like chasing the wind.
> —*Ecclesiastes 4:4 GNT*

You will actually be well *ahead* of the Jones' if, while both Jones parents are out working, you spend your time enjoying a pleasing forty-five-minute walk with your family or an afternoon picnicking with them on the grass. Rather than the other way around, the Jones' just might notice *you* are living the robust and fulfilling lifestyle.

No one enjoys greater influence on your child's thinking than you do. That is unless, of course, you are not available to spend time with your child. In that case, the television, video games, Internet, or an individual other than her parent provides direction for her.

It is not wise to leave your child's upbringing to chance. Unless you are a single parent or suffer some dire circumstance, I cannot imagine monetary income being so valuable that your child should be subjected to less than your greatest parenting effort, which means, *minimally*, spending substantial time with her.

Everybody today seems to be in such a terrible rush; anxious for greater developments and greater wishes and so on; so that children have little time for their parents; parents have little time for each other; and the home begins the disruption of the peace of the world.

—*Mother Teresa*

Parents, in this modern-day atmosphere of apparent need to acquire the latest and most sophisticated technology, toys, and pleasures, please do not lose sight of your most pertinent responsibility, and joy: that of training your child. That responsibility can be accomplished only by being there.

Education

As parents, you and your spouse have primary responsibility for educating your children. However, since you cannot expect to know everything relevant to education, you must entrust trained educational professionals to assist you.

As the parents' assistants, teachers are proprietors of the second most important responsibility in the world. Parents first, teachers second.

We teachers can only help the work going on, as servants wait upon a master.
—*Maria Montessori*

When a conflict arises between teacher and student, some parents automatically side with their child. These parents often don't seem to care what the real story is; they only want to help their child out of trouble. That is a sad perspective. That sort of parent does not realize they and the teacher are in a joint effort with the same common goal.

Is education expensive? We have all heard the phrase, "If you think education is expensive, try ignorance."

To be blind is bad, but worse is to have eyes and not see.
—*Helen Keller*

A well-rounded and useful (and used) education does not cost; it pays rewards and benefits. There are copious amounts of data displaying the fact that earnings generally increase with attainment of higher levels of formal education.

The increase in employment opportunity and potential dollar return offers but a portion of the benefit realized by increased knowledge. The educated mind, with more avail of possibilities, enjoys greater expectations in all aspects of vitality. Being learned provides a greater sense of personal worth and provides genuine cause for added optimism.

Wisdom

Knowledge and wisdom, is there a difference?

You can obtain a general knowledge of many different subjects and, for the most part, that general knowledge gets you by in life. But you'll receive greater economic value by acquiring an area of specialized knowledge, rather than merely a general knowledge. In other words, get *good* at something.

If you become better at something than most people are, other people will pay you for your knowledge and expertise. That is assuming, of course, that you are willing to go to work and offer to apply your specialized knowledge in some way.

If you attain both a general knowledge *and* an area of specialized knowledge, people will think you are really something. And people will be right, too.

Now if you take all that knowledge you have acquired and assemble it all together in your mind in an orderly fashion, then you *might* attain a level of being a wise person.

**It is easier to get older than
it is to get wiser.**[6]

You cannot gain wisdom without first acquiring knowledge. But simply having done a lot of "book learning" will not automatically give you wisdom. If it were that simple, we would have a world filled with many wise people.

Knowledge is all around us. Wisdom is not.

**Never mistake knowledge for wisdom.
One helps you make a living;
the other helps you make a life.**
—*Sandra Carey*

In chapter four, we explored the concept of seeking truth and understanding. In order to attain wisdom, you need to employ the skills of discovering both real truth *and* understanding.

How can you gain wisdom if you are accepting as "truth" things that are not even factual? And if you *do* believe what is authentically correct but are not able to perceive *why* it is so, you may be easily convinced by some fast-talking, not-so-wise fake guru that she is right, and you didn't really know what you thought you knew after all. In other words, your knowledge would be frail and without credible conviction, not nearly adequate enough for a person to acquire the status of being a wise one.

> **To acquire knowledge,**
> **one must study;**
> **but to acquire wisdom,**
> **one must observe.**
> —*Marilyn vos Savant*

Is chronological age a factor in acquiring wisdom? Well, it does take time to learn what needs to be beneficially filtered in or out of the brain and to assemble all the input in a superior fashion. So, yes, from the standpoint that acquiring wisdom takes time, age is a factor.

However, that is not to say that most well-aged brains have become wise. Or that no middle-aged people have acquired such status. It can, however, be said with certainty that no six-year-old wise gurus exist.

Only a very small percentage of all people acquire the revered status of being a wise intellectual.

CHAPTER 7

THE WORKPLACE

The vast majority of us have not been born into massive amounts of money. We are forced to take a job for income so we can pay our living expenses.

If that is your condition, you have a lot of good company in that regard. Because you are forced to work does not mean you have to be one of those people who associates "work" with drudgery.

Work can be enjoyable and, at times, downright fun. Joy in your work comes through joy in your attitude, the same as with anything you are involved with in life. Even though you may work out of necessity, you will do well to find a job that doesn't *feel* like work to you, by doing something you enjoy.

**There is work that is work
and there is play that is play;
there is play that is work
and work that is play.
And in only one of these lie happiness.**

—Gelett Burgess

There is no rationale for taking or keeping a job that lessens your quality of life.

Motivate and Become Motivated

Have you ever had a supervisor who didn't have a clue when it came to making the workplace a fun and motivating environment? I'm sure almost all of us have. And that's unfortunate. She just doesn't quite seem to understand that when people are pumped and enjoying what they do, workers produce better.

I recall the challenge of working with one such individual while employed in a retail store. As a shift supervisor and support person for management, she was expected to physically work with, and at the same time, motivate and boost morale of, her fellow employees. She stocked shelves as well as anyone; however, she simply could not acquire sensitive understanding and the ability to motivate others.

She believed work should be just that: work, drudgery, not fun. She found little room for finding pleasure in working.

When approached by one of her coworkers on possibly making things a little more pleasant and fun, and spicing up the work environment as enjoyed under the previous supervisor, this particular management support member was not at all receptive.

She huffed, "When I come to work, I expect to *work* for a full eight hours. I don't expect to have fun when I come here. I *earn* what the company pays me."

That individual had no business being promoted to any level of management. She was a physically hard worker but unable to motivate others to a level of greater proficiency. She held no concept of building a productive and inspired team.

> **Men can be stimulated**
> **to show off their good qualities**
> **to the leader who seems to think**
> **they have good qualities.**
> —*John Richelsen*

The greatest asset any business has is happy and productive employees. Employees convey their attitudes to fellow employees *and* to customers. When the spirit is drained from an employee, she becomes a liability rather than an asset to the company. Businesses can ill afford any employee who feels unproductive and unappreciated.

In another job, one of my first as a young adult, the company supervisor had a real handle on motivating employees and making the workplace fun.

I worked in a factory producing bottled beverages. As you might suspect, it was normally tedious work.

However, the plant manager found a way to challenge us. He promised he would take out the whole plant's workforce for a noon lunch at company expense if we set a new production record. We became motivated. All were determined to beat our old record. In fact, we set a new standard for ourselves four times in the following six weeks! Every day we were striving to do our very best.

The plant manager appreciated our accomplishments and made sure we knew it.

Did our extra effort benefit the company? You bet. And we employees, even on the days we were not successful in attaining our goal of setting a new record, certainly benefited as well. We enjoyed a new camaraderie in working together toward a common goal. The normal drudgery of that factory line transformed for us!

Leaders are Servants

One's quest for fulfilling joy becomes accomplished primarily through serving others.

In general, those who serve best in the workforce become the workers considered for promotion to management. Some ineffectual leaders accept their new position as a status of power with a sense of pride and a show of authoritarian muscle flexing. The reality of the situation is, by accepting a promotion, they agreed to indenture themselves to serving others to an even greater degree than before.

Executives promoting someone to a position of authority without training that new manager to sense a deeper and more intense attitude of servitude miss an important detail. The newly promoted supervisor typically gets taught details of her new job tasks except for the all-important element of how to effectively *serve* subordinates.

The ideal manager empowers others. She takes a keen interest in listening to others and encouraging workers' input.

Those supervisors, managers, and other lead persons able to make the transition from serving their superiors to serving their subordinate coworkers will be respected. In the process of gaining respect, the leaders themselves naturally earn greater authority.

A real leader accepts blame for her team's faults and quickly passes credit to others rather than take all the credit herself.

The Security of a Paycheck

Does that steady paycheck really offer security?

Anyone who experienced an unwanted loss of employment felt the sense of having their security blanket yanked out of their grasp. That condition creates a feeling of anxiety for any normal person. Even though you may not have particularly appreciated the work environment, or your position within the company while you had it, your sense of certainty and comfort has been jilted. And it doesn't feel good.

You may even find yourself yearning for a retrieval of that position that just a few weeks ago felt so stifling to you.

A long-time employee of a large oil company suddenly found himself in the unsettling position of being forced to decide between two choices, neither of which was satisfactory to him. He could transfer to a new location with the company and accept a lower position, or he could be laid off. As frightening as it was for the gentleman, he chose to be laid off.

The company he worked for was huge. As long as he had been in their employ, the company offered him a sense of security. The company was like family to him, cared about him, and took care of him.

When an economic crunch happened along, the "family" dumped him out on the street to fend for himself. So much for security!

Surprisingly to himself, he did not fall into oblivion. In fact, with time he came to realize the company had unwittingly given him a great gift by letting him go—freedom.

He chose a whole new career direction. To his delight, he discovered he liked writing books and helping others realize their own potential. He has been soaring ever since.

He was fortunate that the large oil company pulled his stifling sense of security and steady paycheck away from him. Had that not happened, this gentleman would likely today still be giving part of the fruits of his efforts to a large company for *their* growth and his feeling of "security."

The provider of his steady and secure paycheck offered him a feeling of security as long as it benefited the company. As soon as that changed, his security vanished into thin air.

Remember, there is no security in this world, there is only opportunity.

Entrepreneurs, inventors, and innovators make up a distinctive sector of humanity. They step out and take risks the majority of us dare not take. Most entrepreneurs understand the dole from an employer does not offer security, but rather represents personal limitation. Innovators choose the challenge of betterment as their stimulation and master.

The daring innovators in our world hold much influence in direction for the rest of humanity. The invention and subsequent mass production of automobiles, the discovery and utilization of electricity, and the invention of computers rank among the most prevalent examples of influence in your life today.

Just Do It

Just do it. Do it now! Get started. There is a positive power acquired by beginning. The act of beginning initiates momentum.

**The real fulfillment begins
as soon as you get on your way.**
—*Ralph S. Marston, Jr.*

When I first came up with the idea of writing this book, I had few ideas and no real plan in mind. Initially, I had the vague and uncertain feeling that attempting to write my first book would be a challenge, and, at the same time, would likely be something I would find personal pleasure in doing.

Like all ideas, this one could easily escape if I did not develop some conviction toward it.

I wanted to begin. So I sat down at my computer and simply started writing. A few days later, I stopped writing, and *then* began the planning process for this new book!

**Take the first step in faith.
You don't have to see the whole staircase,
just take the first step.**
—*Martin Luther King, Jr.*

The act of getting started quickly silenced any doubts or fears I felt as to whether I could handle a project as large and time-consuming as writing a book. My first doubts soon turned into confidence. I discovered writing a book was even more enjoyable than I imagined it would be.

> **If you hear a voice within you
> say 'you cannot paint,'
> then by all means paint,
> and that voice will be silenced.**
> —*Vincent Van Gogh*

I took the first step, that of beginning. The delicate thought began to take on physical shape, which now made it more difficult to throw aside.

Do What You Love

If you work in a job you do not appreciate, strictly for the paycheck, you are not getting paid enough. When working at a job you love, a job you find fulfillment and pleasure in doing, you won't feel like you're working. But you can still *call* it work if you want.

> **I never had a job.
> I always played baseball.**
> —*Satchel Paige*

When you enjoy the fulfilling situation of getting paid for doing what you find pleasure in doing, the money you earn becomes secondary.

If you need to accept a cut in pay to do what you enjoy, then accept the lower financial reward for now. You may have to give something up initially for the more significant reward later. But, you will still be ahead of the game, even right now, because fulfillment in your life is *not* about the money you make. Your life is about growth and development and the thrill you get in living. Your happiness depends on enjoying today and enjoying this very moment.

**Choose a job you love,
and you will never have to work
a day in your life.**
—*Confucius*

Besides, when you find work that is truly fun for you, you have an excellent chance of pulling ahead of the rest of your colleagues. If you enjoy doing it, you tend to perform well. That condition is likely to secure a pay raise for you, eventually making the cut in pay you previously accepted a non-event. You just might find yourself enjoying your "work" and being rewarded with *more* money for doing it.

As creative enjoyment flows *from* you, often the resulting creation converts to monetary wealth flowing *toward* you.

You receive financial reward *and* have fun!

**Success means getting to do what you
really want to do in your work life
and your love life, doing it very well, and
feeling good about the fact that you're doing it.**
—*Lou Tice*

Get Good at Something

In doing what you enjoy, focus in one or two areas. It is imprudent to try to be good at many things. That exercise simply allows you to become *mediocre* at many things. You do well for yourself, and others, to get good at something and do that something better than most people do it.

There is a quote that has been attributed to two different men, Andrew Carnegie and Mark Twain. "Put all your eggs in one basket, then watch that basket." I'm not sure which of these great men deserves credit for the original quote, but the principle of the quote contains merit.

The catchy phrase, however, goes against the grain of what the masses of common people accept as wise counsel.

You may note here that these two great men of meritorious character evidently agreed in the doctrine of putting all your eggs in one basket. What they believed was not the same conventional wisdom we hear so often—that diversification is a prudent practice. In fact, their belief was the exact opposite.

Consider the correlation that each of these men agreed with this principle of *un*-common sense and that each of these great men also excelled in their respective professions. They were able to recognize the folly of conventional wisdom and common sense the ordinary masses chose to adopt as "truth."

Living to Serve Others

When your Creator created you in his likeness, he built into your hard drive a desire to serve. This is *the* major component of your "Divine Design." Sharing your time and your possessions with another person, and the recipient's display of appreciation toward you, give you a sense of genuine satisfaction.

No member of any family, any business, indeed any human relationship, prospers without practicing the law of serving others.

> **If you contribute
> to other people's happiness,
> you will find the true good,
> the true meaning of life.**
> —*His Holiness, the Dalai Lama*

A relationship can survive for a while, but it will never flourish without the two-way interaction of caring for and serving each other. That pertains to *all* relationships including between two individuals, between business and employee, or business and customer.

Imprudent people seek pleasure and self-indulgence as their main objective. When people become selfish and do things only for their own enjoyment, the search for joy backfires. They find themselves unfulfilled in the end.

> **We are not put on this earth for ourselves,
> but are placed here for each other.**
> —*Jeff Warner*

Make it your very purpose in life to assist others and to recognize the good within everyone you meet. Especially, assist others in bringing out their own good qualities, thereby further increasing their potential. As a side benefit, that effort on your part increases your own potential and resourcefulness; the grantor of a good deed always gains at least as much as the recipient does.

> **It is one of the most beautiful**
> **compensations of life that**
> **no man can sincerely try to help another**
> **without helping himself.**
> —*Ralph Waldo Emerson*

When Sam Walton first began his Wal-Mart retail business, he strove to obtain the very lowest cost of the store's merchandise by purchasing in large quantities. Unlike the typical retailer who secured a piece of merchandise at a discounted cost, Mr. Walton chose to pass his savings on to his customers. Not only was that a good way to serve others, Mr. Walton soon discovered it was also a great business practice. Customers appreciated the unusually low prices and spread the word. More customers came. Mr. Walton was then able to purchase in even larger quantities and receive even greater discounts on the cost of his stores' merchandise. He continued to pass along the additional savings rather than keep them for himself.

The company Sam Walton founded grew to become the largest retailer in the world. The idea of serving others worked for him. No real surprise there.

The concept of serving others benefits you in your personal relationships as well as well as it works in business.

> **You can have everything in life you want
> if you will just help enough other people
> get what they want.**
> —*Zig Ziglar*

By acquiring the desire to live in true servitude to others, you gain a peripheral benefit. You naturally acquire the feeling of benevolent love toward, and from, your human fellowship. That is a huge and powerful alliance.

People who learn to serve others well acquire a status of high distinction in this world.

> **Whoever wants to be great
> must become a servant.**
> —*Mark 10:43 TM*

America, the Mosaic

We are fortunate to be a nation of people with varied and diverse cultural backgrounds. Most people living in the United States either have ancestors or have themselves come to "the New World" to partake in the resulting cultural fusion of America.

We learn something from the peoples of each culture. Each offers a unique perspective.

My wife and I both have ancestry who came from Europe to America in the nineteenth and twentieth centuries. During that time, immigrants coming from certain

countries and cultures were persecuted as being undesirable to southwestern Minnesota. These new foreigners
thought differently, and preferred different ways of doing
things than most "native" people living in this area. Most
people living here weren't *actually* native to this part of
the country, or even to *any* part of this country; yet they
were here longer than the new immigrants, so felt this
land somehow belonged to them.

With time, the newer immigrants came to be accepted.
The old and the new cultures merged to a large degree.
Belgians, Irish, Polish, Icelanders, Germans, Norwegians,
Swedes, and more, eventually began to intermingle
together. People shared ideas and cultural practices, and
eventually melded into one new culture of people.

In recent years we again see a new influx of immigrants to northern regions of the United States. Hispanics,
Hmongs, East Indians, and Somalis are all relatively new
to the region. Racial-based murmuring can sometimes be
heard. "They are different."

How quickly and so easily people forget what their
own ancestors had to go through when they first came to
the New World.

We, as a nation of workers, have become somewhat
spoiled and unwilling to always do that which needs to be
done in order for a business to prosper. New immigrants
are often willing to accept work considered "beneath" the
average American worker. If an immigrant is willing to do
what benefits society, then she is good for America.

The United States is a mixture of many diverse cultures. Let us celebrate and welcome new additions!

Retirement

Choosing to retire from serving in the workplace can be a scary thing for many individuals. Retiring creates a substantial change in lifestyle. This change usually occurs at a time in life when resistance to change is a favored sentiment. So despite the expected joy retirement can bring, retirement also produces unwelcome stress.

Retirement should be a time of reinvigoration, a new beginning. You are changing from the routine of committing forty hours every week to employment to exploring new possibilities and possibly new interests.

That is exciting! Retirement is no time to get bogged in a state of depression or fear. You are now useful in new ways that weren't available when you previously committed forty hours a week to working. As long as you are willing to serve your Creator or fellow man in some way, you have purpose and value.

Take the dream you've been putting off and experience it now!

If you choose, upon retirement, to *finally* do that work which you truly enjoy, you may become more fulfilled and useful than you ever were in your working career.

After Harlan "Colonel" Sanders retired, he decided to play with a secret herb mixture he concocted for baking chicken. He had so much fun with it that his renewed hobby turned into a new business. He made his fortune *after* retiring from his job!

During your earning years, you spend approximately one-third of your non-sleeping hours working for income. In terms of time, that is a *huge* investment. Considering time itself is one of your most valuable assets, it behooves you to make certain your time spent "working" is pleasurable for you.

CHAPTER 8

MONEY

Money is a unit of measure for value. Hours measure time, degrees measure temperature, inches and miles measure distance. Dollars measure tangible value.

Money is an inanimate tool created by man to benefit man. Money is a representative form of value for all material things and performed services transferred between people. Because the value of any material good or service can be converted down to a paper bill or a metal coin, money becomes the most pure form, the most concentrated state, of materialism.

Money has become tied to our very existence simply through the sheer number of financial transactions necessary in our daily lives. Considering the frequent handling of money necessary in our normal daily activity, it is amazing how many people choose to remain unlearned in the subject of money management.

**Most people spend more time
planning their vacations
than their financial future.[7]**

Even if money holds little interest for you, you will benefit by understanding some basic principles of money management.

Financial management is the same as virtually all disciplines of life. When you pay attention to your larger financial picture and handle major financial considerations responsibly, you become allowed to enjoy smaller moments in your life without financial concern. Then your moments as you live can be better appreciated for their *own* worth.

Less Can Be More

Modern science and technology help create people's desire for more and more material things. I am certainly not postulating that science and new innovation are a bad thing. But, you must be vigilant of what effect they cause on your desires. A simple life unburdened by excessive physical possessions and desire for possessions holds much merit.

> **The man who is content with nothing possesses all things.**
> —*Nicolas Boileau-Despreaux*

Let us compare two people of wealth. One is a multi-billionaire. She feels somewhat frustrated because she always keeps busy trying to procure "the next big deal" and watching the many aspects of her great financial empire, and retains little time for herself. The other is a gentleman who thinks of nothing more enjoyable than taking his grandchildren out fishing on a quiet day. In fact, he does that very thing whenever he can, which is often. The multi-billionaire is wealthy in her many possessions; the grandfather is wealthy in his simple pleasures.

Which of these people do you feel has more wealth? Consider why you chose the person you did. And how does *your own* life measure against your choice?

If you are not happy with the content of your life, more money and more possessions will not enhance the meaning of your existence. They could even magnify your feeling of frustration or discontent.

Money is a Tool

Because money is a tool, it should become a slave to its possessor, just as a vacuum cleaner, lawn mower, or a set of wrenches is a slave, or tool, to its owner. Unfortunately, most people envision money backwards. Money does not end up empowering them; rather, they choose to become enslaved *to* money.

> **Money is a good servant**
> **but a bad master.**
> —*French proverb*

When you work at a job you dislike simply for the money, you make yourself a slave to money. A slave to unfeeling and uncaring money, no less.

People learn how to work for money, but many remain uneducated in how to make money work for them. Most people spend much time and effort trying to balance their earning and spending of money, and most of that time and effort is consumed by *earning* money. Take control and make money start working for *you*.

Your life isn't *about* money. Your life is no more about money than your life is about a saw, a hammer, or an automobile. They all are merely tools to make your life easier and more productive.

Money by itself can never make anyone happy or miserable. There is nothing in its nature that achieves that capability. By the same token, money is neither good nor bad; money is used by its possessor for benefit or regression. The money's owner merely makes her own choices about whether to do good or bad with it.

> **Money does not pay for anything,**
> **never has, never will.**
> —*Albert Jay Nock*

The application of money may purchase an enviable education that can create a more beautiful world. Or, on the other hand, the application of money could be misused in the brainwashing and training of people, creating the desire to cause useless and unnecessary pain to others through terroristic activities.

Similarly, a sense of financial wealth or insufficiency is merely a mental perspective. What one person perceives to be an abundance, another may perceive to be an insignificant tally. Yet the physical condition of money and the amount of dollars will be the same for each person.

Having at least *some* money at your disposal becomes a pragmatic necessity in today's world. However, the extreme of possessing *too much* discretional money poses potential to help you destroy the values you need for enjoying a robust and fulfilling life.

Mentality Toward Money

Many people develop unhealthy attitudes and thoughts about money.

Some spend money like it carries no value. They seem to want to unload their wallet or their checking account just as quickly as they can. For whatever reason, they choose to put their money back into circulation and the sooner the better.

Maybe worse is the person who thinks money is all-powerful, something to cling onto. She could not spend it even if money possessed the capability of saving her soul. So ultimately, she someday passes into the next world and leaves almost everything she worked and scrimped for so someone else can squander it.

Both extremes are sad predicaments for any mind to be poisoned with.

Some people look with disdain on those who possess significant amounts of money. What's with that? Do they feel there is no hope for themselves to ever reach a significant level of prosperity in their own lives? Is it mere jealousy?

They regard the power of wealth as being a bad thing. However, power is a *wonderful* tool as long as the power is possessed by someone of character willing to perform good deeds. So, wealth holds a purpose *higher* than being merely a medium of exchange. Financial wealth is a beneficial tool to be used for conveying good works in this world.

Possessors of monetary wealth must, however, remain ever vigilant to keep their wealth productive and pure in purpose. Misuse of wealth can destroy a person of weak character.

An Unfortunate Lesson from Our Past

Many of us know or knew someone who lived in the time of the Great Depression, the 1930s. What comes to your mind when you think of people who lived through that period?

Stop here for a moment and give the thought some consideration.

I think it fair to assume you came up with the tight-fisted, money-scrimping habits of that generation of people.

Many good and valuable lessons came out of the trauma of that economic fiasco. But, sadly, so many people, with an abundance of God-given capabilities and a wealth of goodness within, became deeply embedded with the mentality of lack.

> **Men are not prisoners of fate,**
> **but only prisoners**
> **of their own minds.**
> —*Franklin D. Roosevelt*

The lesson was so intense and so widespread that frugality became a lifelong habit for almost the entire generation of American people who experienced the Great Depression. Even for those who, later in their lifetime, accumulated a comfortable financial independence for themselves, most were unable to spend their money and appreciate the benefit afforded by their previous thrifty ways.

Being broke is a temporary situation.
Being poor is a mental state.
—*Mike Todd*

The massive affliction with the feeling of lack in so many people, *not* the hard economic times, ultimately became the greatest tragedy of the Great Depression!

Make Money Secondary

When contemplating choices, financial cost should be a secondary consideration—unless, of course, you have an insufficiency of money. If it happens to be in short supply for you, money may necessarily become a *primary* consideration in your life. That is a sad condition. Make every effort to overcome the debilitating condition of needing money just "to make ends meet" in your life.

The condition of having limited financial resources thwarts freedom to live your life as you *choose*. Incidentally, the opposite extreme of possessing too much money also holds the same potential. Determine what level of financial position is correct in your life and then, simply stated, *attain* that level.

Choose to make life for yourself a daring adventure based not on monetary concerns, but on what is truly meaningful for you.

Poverty Is a Mind Condition

Poverty is a self-limiting condition of the mind caused by predominantly thinking of lack. It is a debilitating condition.

> **To view poverty simply as an economic condition,**
> **to be measured by statistics,**
> **is simplistic, misleading and false;**
> **poverty is a state of mind...**
> —*Patrick J. Buchanan*

Your way of thinking naturally moves toward your future way of thinking. That is, your thought at this moment in time spreads to your thought occurring in the next moment.

Your thinking about lack becomes part of a vicious cycle going on in your mind. Your thinking of lack keeps feeding on itself, and soon becomes your predominant focus. When that pitiful condition exists, only predominately negative notions pass through your brain filter. As your mind naturally gravitates toward that which it focuses on, you *intensify* the mental image of being a person who is lacking.

> **If you are going to let the fear**
> **of poverty govern your life...**
> **your reward will be that you eat,**
> **but you will not live.**
> —*George Bernard Shaw*

Abundance, by the exact same process, only in reverse, comes to you through noble and charitable thinking. To enjoy abundance, focus thought on your abundance and your generosity, rather than on what you lack.

**The more abundance that is
lived, experienced and appreciated,
the more there is to go around.**
—*Ralph S. Marston, Jr.*

Don't Give a Handout, Teach

Individuals are generally better able to do for themselves than any government can. Except for developing a sound national infrastructure, the individual citizenry will almost always be more efficient than an impersonal and uncaring government, both in cost of dollars and in productivity.

No one maintains more interest in your personal welfare than you do yourself. No government, no insurance company, no large corporation, not even a small one- or two- or three-employee business.

That means only *you* can effectively improve your lot in life. A freebie handout without obligation is exactly the wrong medicine to take when seeking self-improvement.

**Give a man a fish;
you have fed him for a day.
Teach a man to fish:
and you have fed him for a lifetime.**
—*Old Chinese proverb*

In order to retain a healthy self-respect, you must also hold a feeling of self-adequacy. Repeated acceptance of a free, no obligation handout from a stranger, or a government, is detrimental to your mental wealth. It does bad things to your mind and your feeling of self-worthiness.

> ## You can't get rid of poverty
> ## by giving people money.
> —*P. J. O'Rourke*

A shiftless wino on the street will not improve her lot through obtaining money or a free bottle of wine. No, she needs a new and different mindset. The previous bottles she obtained helped her get to the point she is at today. She does not need any more reinforcement of being that person.

She needs re-programming of her subconscious mind and rehabilitation of her physical addiction, *not* a physical handout. She needs to be re-created from within.

> ## The greatest good you do for another
> ## is not just to share your riches
> ## but to reveal to him his own.
> —*Benjamin Disraeli*

Wealth Is a Mindset

When you think healthy thoughts, more healthy thoughts tend to proliferate. Success breeds greater future successes. Your increased achievement makes the next level of capability more accessible for you. Robust, healthy, abundant thinking brings prosperity. Wealthy is healthy!

Until you are able to accept that as a truth in your mind, the process toward financial prosperity cannot begin for you. Those who despise people of affluence, who make negative remarks about wealth, and believe abundance can never be theirs have something in store for themselves. Their resulting condition is a product of what they think.

What about the verse from the Bible (I Timothy 6:10 KJV) which reads, "For the love of money is the root of all evil"? According to John-Roger and Peter McWilliams in their book entitled *Life 101*[8], this verse before translation to either Greek or English, reads closer to "lust for money" rather than the words "love for money."

Love, being a fond feeling or affection, and lust, being a desire for indulgence, are two very different things. Remember, money merely characterizes the purest condensed form of material goods and physical services. The Biblical verse implies "indulgence for material possessions and indulgence of corporeal acts as being the root of all evil." Who can argue with that? That statement makes perfect sense.

So the verse does not mean wealthy people are doomed to an eternity of damnation in hell. No, it means all people of a lustful and greedy nature might want to reconsider their ways. Certainly there are many people possessing financial wealth who love God, serve their fellow man, and help create a better world.

Your Money Isn't You

Most people consider their financial matters taboo for discussion. Many feel more comfortable sharing information on their private sex lives than their financial situation. They act as if their financial condition is somehow sacred information, and divulging such information exposes themselves to scrutiny that reveals a most classified and personal secret.

Consider also: to many people, their degree of financial success or failure becomes reflective of how they choose to assess their personal worth in this world. However, **how you live, how you love, how you serve and appreciate those around you, are the essential qualities that make your life worthy.** Your money is not a part of you. Its value is quite limited when compared to your thinking and subsequent actions.

> **There are people who have money and people who are rich.**
> —*Coco Chanel*

Don't Watch Your Pennies

Cautiously watching how you spend your nickels and pennies will not be beneficial to your well-being. In fact, it will hurt you. Being a penny-pinching miser helps form the creation of a feeling of lack. You simply cannot afford to harbor that thought in your mind.

Your money management effort is better utilized tending to your larger and more significant financial picture.

Along the same vein, it is generally not worth your time to tend to trivial matters. And small change *is* a trivial matter. Your time is always of greater value than your small change. Develop a sense of worthiness within— worthiness of self and worthiness of your time. Do not get bogged down in the small change mentality.

**Most people fail in life because
they major in minor things.**
—*Tony Robbins*

Time is Not Money

You have heard the saying "time is money." It is not. *Use* of your time procures money either through your effort or investment, but time itself is not money. It is not even close.

Your time holds *far* more value than your money does. You wouldn't trade your life, or even half your life, for all the money in the world, would you?

**Waste your money and
you're only out of money,
but waste your time and
you've lost a part of your life.**
—*Michael Leboeuf*

The time you have is limited. You only get a certain amount of it.

Money, on the other hand, is not limited. Your government prints as much money as there is a call for. The only limitation for you is how much of the infinite supply you demand for your endeavors.

Money does not make money. Neither does money produce income any more than a saw builds a house. Thought, followed with action, produces monetary gain.

The person who possesses money for investment uses money merely as a tool to assist her.

Financial Debt

Having credit available to you can be a liberating condition. Conversely, owing debt can be a stifling condition.

Because credit is relatively easy to obtain these days, many of us choose to use credit as a way of life. Recognize, there is good reason lending institutions encourage you to borrow money from them, and it's not because they are looking out for *your* well-being.

Think of getting a loan as being a debt to someone else, since that's exactly what it is. And realize the lender expects you to pay the money back, plus interest. You now become obligated to pay another monthly payment.

Debt to someone else: why on earth would anyone want to burden themselves with that consciousness? To be in debt, financially or in *any* capacity for that matter, is confining and very *un*-liberating. Your awareness of obligation to someone takes away a freedom. You become indebted to another. Indebtedness is not a very good feeling for you.

> **The rich rule over the poor,**
> **and the borrower is the slave of the lender.**
> —*Proverbs 22:7 NRSV*

Now that you are indebted, you *must* trudge off to work. You are working for three entities now. You work for the company or customer who employs you, for yourself, and now for the lender. By taking on this new obligation, you willfully choose to become a slave to your lender for a part of each workday.

That burden will hang with you until you eventually release yourself from being indebted to another.

Use Credit Only for Benefit

Despite the shackles a debt imposes on your mind, for the wise and prudent money manager, borrowing other people's money *can* sometimes be good for you.

A useful rule to consider adopting for your own good is: use credit only to purchase what you expect to be an *appreciating* asset. There are many examples of investments that have a strong likelihood of going up in value. Of course, the expected gain must be higher than the expected interest cost to qualify as a wise investment.

Owning your own residence offers one of the foremost beneficial investments most people can make. Since you need to live *somewhere* anyway, and real estate pricing usually trends upward, it makes sense to own your home rather than rent it. Paying out a monthly rent payment only helps your landlord enjoy the financial benefits of real estate ownership.

An appreciating asset would likely *not* include a car, sofa, or electronic device. Cars, sofas, and electronic devices almost always go down in value. As your indebtedness for the car decreases, so does the value of the car. In the end, you own nothing. And when the car dies, you probably get to start looking all over again for a different car and another loan.

It makes greater sense to buy only what you can afford, what you have cash for. When it comes to debt, it's really not much fun keeping up with the neighbors.

Be smart. Use credit wisely or not at all. If you cannot be responsible with money and debt, do *not* use credit at all.

An exception to the rule: another time when using credit may benefit you is when an emergency arises that you are financially unprepared for, such as a health issue for you or a loved one. Despite the burden of financial indebtedness it brings, the situation likely offers greater value to you than any money concerns.

Is Your Car for Transportation?

It seems virtually everyone owns her own personal mode of transportation. It's part of present-day Americana.

What goes into a decision as to what is the best automobile for you to own? Quite obviously, for most people of modern times, an automobile represents more than being something able to get them from point A to point B. Any little vehicle that has an engine, wheels, and a place to park your derriere is capable of that much. But nothing that utilitarian can be found on the roads today. Air conditioning, automatic transmission, and power brakes have all become standard equipment. We don't think twice about those luxuries. Our vehicles keep getting more and more cushy. And no one today would consider purchasing a vehicle without a radio.

Most of us *always* buy a vehicle that is more than merely a mode of transportation. Just gotta have the entertainment center on the dash, power windows, or the sunroof. After all, other people will be seeing you in your "home-away-from-home." For many, their car becomes a symbolic expression of who they are, and they are very willing to borrow whatever funds necessary to call that more-than-they-can-afford vehicle their own.

How you choose to spend your resources impacts how enslaved you become to money. Our choice of automobile has become the most extravagant depreciating asset we get coerced into by our need for peer approval. It doesn't even take a smooth talking salesperson to convince us. Many of us go into the showroom *already* convinced that a showpiece is what we desire and we are willing to borrow the funds to get it. And it generally does not take much pressure from a salesperson to convince us to raise the ante on what we can spend for this extravagance.

If a wonderful car is truly that important to you, fine; I really am not trying to change your mind in that regard. But be aware this one financial encumbrance, a car costing more money than you have, seems to have become more American to us than baseball, hot dogs, or apple pie. And, if you are like the majority, you are paying through the nose for it.

The luxuries you opt for in life include much more than your choice of transportation. Luxuries are interspersed *throughout* your life. There is a reason most of us have become part of a two-, three-, and even four-job family. And it is *not* because these times are tough. We simply desire more and more.

Who Gets Your Paycheck?

When payday rolls around, do you choose to be on the very *bottom* of the list of people who get to share in the proceeds? If you are like most people, after paying everybody else on the list, you get to keep for yourself what's left over, if there *is* anything left over. That allocation of your paycheck becomes a part of the indebtedness mentality that has so cunningly bombarded this nation.

Rather than holding the traditional "me last" mentality, why not instead adopt a different formula with greater consideration for yourself? Take your net paycheck (after taxes and deductions) and separate it into three allotments.

Number One – 10 percent for the future you

Number Two – 10 percent for charitable causes you consider important

Number Three – 80 percent for you to use now

In that order. Although you remain at the bottom of the list, you don't have to settle for only leftovers. Now, you also climb to the top of the list, right where you belong. You pay yourself first because you earned the paycheck. You are entitled to be first in line to benefit by your effort. If you already have indebtedness from past decisions, the pay back of that indebtedness should for now come out the big part, the 80 percent, until the debt is paid off.

Perhaps you are thinking there is no way you can reasonably cut your paycheck by 20 percent. You may be surprised to find that living on only 80 percent of your current paycheck *is actually quite realistic*. However, if you really think that level would be unmanageable, then change the numbers to something that is workable for you. Maybe change the 80 percent to 90 percent or something similar. But the first two on the list should not be ignored.

The only person who can afford to ignore number one, her future self, is the person who assumes she has little use for financial independence in her future years. Do *not* ignore financial responsibility for your future; if you choose to ignore your future self, you may, in time, find *yourself* on someone's list as number two, a charitable cause.

Likewise, trying to live a worthy and fulfilling life of your own, while at the same time choosing to *ignore* your needy brethren, comprises two incompatible standards. Since giving and sharing of yourself and your resources gives your life meaning and worthiness, you cannot afford to ignore the second allotment, giving to others.

We make a living by what we get, but make a life by what we give.
—*Winston Churchill*

The Benefit of Beginning Early

You probably dream, or perhaps simply assume, that someday in the future you will want to retire from working. Instead of merely dreaming, plan for it.

By implementing the plan just described of paying the future you first, the possibilities for you expand. With time, your life gets easier and more manageable.

Here's an idea that will help in paying the future you. If your place of employment offers direct deposit of your paycheck into a bank account, use it. But do not have your paycheck deposited into your checking account. First, place the money into a *savings* account, then withdraw the 80 percent or 90 percent allotted for your current use. The benefit to this method is you get to touch only what is yours now. By keeping your future resources separate, you lessen the temptation to take and spend them now.

Years ago, I implemented a plan very similar to this one. I can tell you from my own experience, it is painless once you become used to it. In fact, after only two or three paychecks, you become accustomed to your new living wage. It really and truly is that simple.

When it comes to investing, time is your greatest ally. The sooner you begin investing, the sooner you liberate yourself. Let's look at an eye-opening example here.

Two friends, Sarah and John, were both twenty-one years of age.

Sarah spent money as fast as she earned it. John, however, chose to begin saving for his future right away. He put $2,000 away for investment each year for six years.

After the six years' time, John showed the record of his savings account to Sarah. Sarah calculated that John's total investment had been $12,000 but his account value had already grown to $18,178. John, however, had a change of lifestyle and decided to stop making the annual contribution to his savings account. But he left the accumulated money already in the account to continue its growth.

Sarah thought John's previous investing habit had built quite an impressive figure for such a short time, and she immediately caught the bug. She began investing $2,000 each year. And the bug never left her. After thirty-five years, Sarah, had invested a total of $70,000 of her own money. But now, at the age of sixty-two years, she had an account balance of approximately $960,000!

Sarah had to thank John for showing her the way and perhaps brag a little as well. They began to compare their financial accounts. John, who had invested early in his life, but for only six years, had not wavered in leaving his money in the account to grow for his future.

They were both surprised to realize even though John invested only $12,000 of his own money, his account, as well, was valued at approximately $960,000![9] At age sixty-two, after forty-one years' time, both investors realized a similar-sized nest egg. Almost a million dollars each!

Sarah benefited through years of investing. John benefited by investing early, then letting his money work for him. The earlier you begin, the more time you have to earn interest, thus the more money you will accumulate without having to physically work for it. By consistently leaving your money invested over the years, you earn interest on interest and dividends on dividends, which allows your financial balance to grow *exponentially*.

Time is an extraordinary element in this formula for financial security.

As a youngster you are forced to work for your money. Then, your invested money works for you. Gaining income from investment offers benefit to the person who wisely manages her time and money. Use the principle yourself. Start paying yourself *now*, the sooner the better.

Time and Risk-to-Reward

Risk is typically perceived as being a scary notion, something to be avoided. But from a practical standpoint, risk offers opportunity. You generally benefit by accepting some risk.

Insurance companies tend to become very wealthy by taking advantage of this principle. People want to eliminate risk and insurance companies collect money to accept risk. People feel secure and the insurance company and its sales agent go to the bank, smiling all the way. Everybody's happy.

You have to accept a degree of risk in everything you do. Walking, driving a car, taking a shower. Indeed, every moment forces at least some risk onto you.

There is always a cost in trying to avoid risk. The premium paid for an insurance policy is merely one example. Another example: one of the safest investments for any investor would be to put her money in a government-insured savings account at any bank. Compare the expected return on that government-insured (very safe) saving account to almost any other investment, and you will find it to be very low in comparison. The difference reflects your cost of risk-avoidance.

> **If you don't risk anything,**
> **you risk even more.**
> —*Erica Jong*

Rather than try to avoid risk (that is futile), learn to manage risk. Learn what constitutes a sensible risk for you to assume and what is not a sensible risk. Then accept only risks that are smart risks. That doesn't mean you will win all the time, but it does mean you are very likely to be a winner in the long run.

The principle of risk management is similar to any other life strategy in that it's prudent to avoid extremes. You can cause unnecessary harm to your financial condition by being either too risk-averse or too receptive to risk.

> **I have learned that**
> **carelessness and over-confidence**
> **are usually far more dangerous**
> **than deliberately accepted risk.**
> —*Wilbur Wright*

Once you gain understanding of accepting and managing risk, you can actually embrace taking sensible risks that are likely to benefit you. Insurance companies and wealth-abounding magnates do not deserve *all* the easy money. Partake in the offering yourself. You deserve it.

An additional benefit to beginning early in paying the future you is, by doing so, you may comfortably utilize a higher risk, higher potential approach to investing.

The benefit of a higher reward is an obvious advantage for you. But, what about the higher risk of loss you must assume in order to obtain that potential?

The advantage of being able to accept a higher risk of loss at a young age is that, should a loss *actually* occur for you, you have many years to make the money back again. If you lose much, or even your entire investment near retirement age, you suffer a more devastating loss. In such occurrence, you would never again in your life be able to take full advantage of the time factor in recouping those losses. Because there is time to make it up, financial ruin at a young age creates less devastation than financial ruin relatively late in life.

Thus, young investors should seek higher potential (higher risk) investments and more mature investors should seek more safe (lower risk) investments. The full benefit of exponential growth is offered *only* to those few wise enough to begin investing early in life.

Receiving a Windfall vs. Earning Your Money

People who think lack often engage in a love-hate relationship with money. They consent to badmouthing the "filthy" rich, then go out and buy $5 or $10 worth of lottery tickets, hoping to win big bucks for themselves. What do you suppose happens when a person of that mentality actually wins the Big One?

I recently came across a couple of statistics. The first statistic cited that more than 90 percent of lottery winners use up their winnings within ten years.

The second statistic related to one particular lottery; 60 percent of the grand prize winners filed bankruptcy within five years of winning! Their ship finally arrived overflowing in abundance and merely ended up buying for them the embarrassing condition of bankruptcy.

What happens in these situations?

In most cases, the winners have been self-sabotaging their minds for years. After investing most years of their lives conditioning their minds to think about their lack of resources, it became virtually impossible to accept the new scenario, abundance.

They received the opportunity to *easily* be financially wealthy but could not make the internal reversal in their thinking. The windfall winners had not gained insight through lessons that come inherently through effort and adversity along the road to obtaining wealth. They held no awareness of the obligations that are a component function of managing financial wealth. Without the corresponding change in their mindset to accept the condition of responsibly handling money, they went out and frivolously spent the unexpected windfall.

If humanity were somehow able to take all the world's money and redistribute it equally, you might think that condition would make for a better world. However, because of our minds' nature, that change would likely not have much long-term effect on the world.

A very large percentage of the same people who in the past learned and used good money management principles to get ahead would once again become the leaders in prolificacy within five to ten years.

Why would that be? Again, because money serves only as an inanimate tool without capabilities of its own, obviously the money itself wouldn't make the difference. The *mental* state of the money's possessor makes virtually all the difference.

Sharing and Giving

There are some things in this world that cannot be appreciated and useful to you unless you give them away. They have no value unless you share them with others. Those things include your time, your talents, your money, and your love. Each of those offers little meaning standing alone.

Perhaps an extreme example here best illustrates the point.

A fine young man of many worldly talents and much financial being suddenly finds himself shipwrecked alone on a small but life-sustainable island.

Suddenly he longs more than ever to be with his young wife and child. How he would also love to see his parents and siblings again. But now, to this unlucky young man, it seems unlikely he will ever be discovered and rescued from his prison of solitude.

He has plenty of time, talent, money, and love here on this island. He's got it all. But he is unable to share any of it.

In his unfortunate predicament, he comes to realize he should have shared all these things more freely while he had the opportunity. He should have released his treasures and let them go. By giving them away, they had value. Now he has these things all to himself, and they are worthless without opportunity to share them.

Give of yourself, share with others, serve others. Live a life of meaning!

CHAPTER 9

RELIGION

Much of this chapter on religion and the entire book is geared toward Christian principles. However, many of the principles taught in Christian doctrine also relate to fundamental doctrine of the world's other major religions. Therefore, all readers may discover truth herein in the intellectual sense of their own faith.

Each of the major religions of the world today proclaims doctrine that inspires human growth and development. Living according to any of their traditional principles bears evidence to the good qualities that lie within humanity. Unfortunately, extreme fanatics surface from time to time with a bizarre new twist from their religion's traditional ethics, giving credence to outsiders of the "wrongfulness" of that particular religion.

Much of what we believe regarding our religion is based, not on logic or provable evidence, but predominately on faith. That inherently gives our belief a state of fragility. *Because* of that fragility, many people hold contempt for the conflicting religious views that others may try to impose on them. There is a fear that if something new makes a bit of sense to them, it might be irreligious to entertain the thought. The new viewpoint could possibly make a dent in their existing belief and somehow be a slight to their Creator. Their fear closes their mind to fresh thinking.

> **A point of view can be a dangerous luxury when substituted for insight and understanding.**
> —*Marshall McLuhan*

Although I choose for myself to believe in Christ and attempt to follow his discipline, I cannot fault anyone for choosing another path toward their ultimate goal. Each of us must decide on the course that is right and most beneficial for herself.

> **True religion is no more and no less than the relationship between man and his God.**
> —*Grace Coolidge*

Faith

Going back to the flat Earth-round Earth example used in chapter three, the very first instant anyone had any inkling the earth might be a big ball rather than being flat, humanity shifted ever so slightly toward a new reality. That truth that we accept today—the earth being a big round ball, rather than the "truth" people previously had filtered in—began its journey of revelation to the common minds.

The new truth, even though existing as only a light twinkling on one mind, replaced the "truth" that anybody with common sense just knew, without a doubt, to be correct.

**Truth always originates in a minority of one,
and every custom begins as a broken precedent.**
—*Will Durant*

"Truth," without understanding, is faith. "Truth," without understanding, may not be actual truth at all. The wide multitude of religious "truths" all have a foundation built on faith, a faith without corporeal understanding. That means my faith is suspect. *Your religious "truth" is suspect as well.*

If you find that assertion disturbing, it could be a good thing. It may mean something just got through your filter that previously had not.

Faith Can be Constricted and Narrow-Minded

One time in my youth, I wrestled with my own religious beliefs. I decided, at someone else's recommendation, to seek the counsel of a particular clergy who was of the same faith I grew up with. The minister was a college professor who studied the teachings and beliefs of major religions of the world. He taught a college class on the major religions' doctrines, as well as atheistic beliefs. In our private session, he told me he was convinced that his and my own religious upbringing was the right one, the proper one. I questioned the fairness of his statement.

Almost all of us grow up being subjected to the religious leanings of our own parents. As such, our parents' basic religious "truths" become, for the most part, enrooted as our own. With time, we may shift a bit from the beliefs of our parents, but the god or gods themselves are generally not open for disputable question.

I asked the minister if, after all his studies, had he instead grown up in India to good parents who ingrained in him the teachings of Hinduism since he was a young lad, did he think he would still feel the same about our own Christian religion today? He said he was sure he would. With that, I considered his answer a biased partiality and gave the minister's counsel little further regard.

Later in life, I did return to believing in the basic religious faith of my childhood. Naturally, however, there were some variations in my adult understanding of the faith versus what I believed as a child.

In another discussion with a fellow Christian, I was informed that obviously Christianity is the real McCoy when it comes to religion because we Christians experience many miracles. I expressed my own view that people of *all* religious faiths experience miracles. After all, a miracle is merely something occurring beyond the humanly understood laws of nature. (More on this in a few pages, under the subtitle *Expect a Miracle*.) He insisted I was quite incorrect in my observation. "Miracles are characteristic of Christianity only." He could not have been more serious about that. That thinking is an example of extreme narrow-mindedness, the sort that stifles any possibility for growth.

Everyone, of any religious belief, and even of *no* religious belief, in fact, every day experiences numerous miracles. Miracles abound all around us in our daily lives. But I suppose this gentleman was likely referring to unusual miracles that are not an everyday occurrence.

Every one of us experiences those as well, the *uncommon* miracles. Even those without faith in *any* religion's teachings experience miracles—occurrences that defy logic or ordinariness.

Caution: Narrow-Mindedness is Dangerous

One night while on a cross-country road trip I had the car radio tuned to a middle-of-the-night talk show. The interview guest was a reformed anti-Jewish extremist. He admitted he performed some foolish acts in his younger days that he presently realized were simply wrong and a demonstration of his juvenile narrow-mindedness.

> **A little knowledge and
> an over-abundance of zeal
> always tends to be harmful.
> In the area involving religious truths,
> it can be disastrous.**
> —*Kathryn Kuhlman*

The thing that stuck with me was when the reformed extremist made the comment, "When you cannot see the opposing viewpoint, when you are 100 percent certain of anything, you are dangerous." Amen to that.

When you are unable to observe the opposing viewpoint with any open-minded objectivity, it is fair to assume you lack wisdom of the subject you are 100 percent certain and, in all probability, have lack of simple factual knowledge on the subject, as well. Once you go beyond the point of holding any degree of objective regard, you develop a prejudice. Prejudiced thinking represents danger imposed by an obstructed brain filter.

Even though you may view someone as narrow-minded or deficient in their thinking, it is not prudent to totally discount their viewpoint. You can disagree and still gain a new perspective. Realizing their perspective furnishes you with a new level of understanding. More understanding automatically gives you potential for additional growth.

Your Faith Should be Beneficial to You

I recently conducted a small and very informal survey. I asked people, "Are humans basically good or are humans basically bad?" I was quite surprised to find that 23 percent of those questioned believed people are "basically bad."

When the answer was "basically bad," I further asked, "Why do you think people are basically bad?" Those "bad" responses were mostly justified by some sort of religious reasoning as their rationale.

For your Creator's sake, and your own, if your religion causes you to accentuate the *bad* qualities in people, change your beliefs! Be assured, God never intended for you to find his creation as being bad or evil. Turn and run as fast as you can! Thinking that man is basically bad is self-defeating and very unhealthy.

Expect a Miracle

Through prayer and expectation, we often obtain desirable outcomes.

Since happenings beyond the humanly understood laws of nature (miracles) occur all the time, doesn't it make sense to *expect* miracles?

Consider the miracle of life and growth. Little bodies in the womb begin as a single cell and divide in a sequential order. Each new cell becomes part of an intestinal wall, or brain component, or fingernail, or hair stem by Nature's design, even *if* humans do not fully comprehend the process.

This common, yet amazing, miracle of organized growth happens in humans, and in all other animal species, big or tiny. It happens in all plant life. This miracle is occurring even in the little microscopic creatures of this world we humans are not aware of.

It's all happening everyday, day after day, whether anyone thinks about it or totally ignores it. That is a wonderful happening beyond the humanly understood laws of nature, truly a miracle.

God is able to, and does, produce miracles copiously and endlessly.

Indeed, what is it for God to create one more wonderful happening beyond human understanding? *Expect* a miracle.

Are You Following a Religious Cult?

Definition of cult: a group or sect whose practices or beliefs are separated from generally accepted values and creeds. The word *cult* most generally conjures up an image of a small fanatical religious following.

If you believe in one of today's major religions, you are following a religion that was, at one time in history, a cult. Each of today's major religions began in a small way and gradually the religion's believers convinced others to follow, believe, and practice the faith with them. With time, the religious following grew in numbers. Today, your major religion is no longer considered a cult because your religious practices or beliefs are generally accepted by a *large* number of people.

Considering the religion you claim as your own was once a new and caustic-to-most-people cult, does that sort of put a different spin on what a cult may be? However, if you are like most people, *your* religion's infancy is something you can be *proud* of. After all, you believe your faith is the correct and proper conviction, and a large number of other people agree with you.

When another person believes in her religion predominately on faith, as do you, her religious faith becomes no less valid than yours. Realizing that faith is based on opinion, and not on absolute fact, someone else's faith is as justifiable and real as your own. You certainly don't have to agree with her but recognize that, as long as the practice of her faith is not harmful to others, she deserves the right to her own thought and her own faith.

The Bible: Symbolic or Literal?

Since the Bible is a documentation of religious faith, I cannot claim *absolute* understanding of its teachings. However, in this section I offer ideas for your consideration to encourage you to think about your own relationship with God and his teachings.

Some Christians accept every word of the Bible in the exact literal way it is written. However, because the Word has varying incongruities, others take the writings of the Bible as symbolic expressions of their religious faith.

Religious scholars today disagree on what teaching was intended in some of the *original* Biblical writings. That is due, at least partly, to the fact that meanings of words and word phrases, in any language, change over the years.

Words have their genealogy, their history... They also have their...social distinctions.

—Virgilia Peterson

The confusion is also partly due to the fact that the written word holds the limitation of lacking direct eye contact, body language, and voice inflection. Meaningful pauses and word emphasis can be easily lost in transposing the spoken word into its written form.

The Bible has not only been translated into many languages today, but it has several varying translations just within the English language alone. Every time something is translated from one language to another the probability exists that something will be transformed in the exchange. Original meanings have been altered, in some cases, many times. Many Biblical translators feel that as modern language changes, so should the latest rendition of the Word.

Jesus, the major principal of the New Testament, very often spoke in a parabolic and metaphoric fashion. He referred to himself as being several manifestations obviously not to be taken in a literal sense, including bread (John 6:35), a rock (I Corinthians 10:4), a gate or door (John 10:9), and a vine (John 15:5).

The verse Matthew 27:5 NCV reads that Judas, a traitor to Jesus, "went off and hanged himself." The verse of Acts 1:18 NCV states in *that* accounting that Judas "fell to his death" in a field, "he burst open and all his insides spilled out."

Are both accountings correct? It is remotely possible, however it appears to be a discrepancy in the recording of the Word. If that is indeed a discrepancy, it can be explained by the symbolic reader as being merely an indication of the *human* imperfection of the scribes, or as the *human* imperfection of subsequent translators.

Religious scholars have posted their stamp of personal approval on which original writings are to be considered as the inspired Word of God. Literal readers of the Word have to further decide for themselves which translated-to-English version, of all the choices available today, is to be incontestable and absolute.

With so many compelling reasons for believing the Word to be a symbolic truth, if you still hold firm to the Bible as a literal word-for-word truth with no room for self-interpretation, your faith is strong—and extreme.

The Evolution Controversy

Are the Bible and scientific teachings of evolution in disagreement? Was the earth, with all its natural splendor and the beginning of the human specie, created in seven short days? In only 168 hours, as the Biblical recordings literally reveal?

The accountings of the Old Testament were for centuries passed down verbally from generation to generation. Only *much later* was the history of our rich earthly heritage recorded in writing. Did original documentation indicate seven days? And if "day" was indeed the term used at the time of recording, was such a day of twenty-four hour duration? Were the historic stories accurately passed by word-of-mouth through centuries of time, without change? If your answer to this last question is yes, do not collect $200, go back to chapter two dealing with change.

God is author of both the Bible and science. Each is bigger than human understanding can fully comprehend. If you find conflict between the Bible and science, it is because you misunderstand one, or more likely, both.

> ### The religion that is afraid of science dishonors God...
> —*Ralph Waldo Emerson*

If you think of the Bible as a symbolic text, the theory of evolution is indeed compatible with the Biblical recording.

Is God Omnipotent?

Genesis 6:6 GNT reads "He (God) was sorry that he had ever made them and put them on the earth. He was so filled with regret."

God? Filled with regret? What's the deal?

Most of us grew up being taught God is all-knowing and not capable of error. Yet, as author of the Good Book, he says he had sorrow and regret for something he had done.

The passage implies to me God does *not* know of everything *before* its actual occurrence. To believe your Creator knows of happenings before their occurrence would mean your Creator knew, even before you were born, what good and bad deeds were to be performed by you in your lifetime. Since it is all pre-determined anyway, you have no responsibility here.

Don't you believe, for one second, *your* life was all determined before birth! Your Creator built into you the ability to make *your own* choices attesting that your life has not been pre-determined for you. He gave you free will. He gave *you* authority to make decisions. He created your free will in his own likeness.

God does, however, know everything you think and do as it occurs.

> **God knows everything I do;**
> **He sees every step I take.**
>
> *—Job 31:4 DRB*

Your Creator has power to be omnipotent, but chose instead to grant authority to *you* in choosing your own self-direction.

I am not implying your Creator is anything less than God. After all, he *is* the Almighty Creator. And, lest you forget, as a sinner and a human, you are lowly in comparison to your Creator.

With your own greatness in mind, *and*, at the same time, a sense of submissive humility toward your Creator, it is wise to keep in mind the truth referred to in I Corinthians 1:25 GNT. It reads, "For what seems to be God's foolishness is wiser than human wisdom, and what seems to be God's weakness is stronger than human strength."

You are built with greatness but Your Creator will always be greater!

Live and Let Live

It is paradoxical that people fight wars and kill other people in the name of religion. How can any religion, believing in a god creator and humanity as creation of their god (or gods), teach that destroying innocent fellow humans is an acceptable practice? Only religious extremists capable of harboring hatred are able to convince *them*selves that human life has such little meaning.

Similarly, when people consider aborting their little ones before birth, they debase the dignity of all humanity. The very fact that abortion is considered verily indicates the little one's physical existence is quite real and indisputable. Some consider the little ones as being lesser than others, or even hold disregard for them as beings *at all*.

As you did it to one of the least
of these my brethren,
you did it to me.
—*Matthew 25:40 RSV*

When I was a young boy, my father and a neighbor were intentionally destroying an old grain storage building on my parents' farm. As the semi-rotten structure was being demolished, my siblings and I caught a bunch of live mice. We imprisoned our captured prey in an old empty water tank.

In retrospect, it was not a very humane way for us to treat other animals.

Nonetheless, I hold memory that, when held in captivity, the pregnant mice gave birth and soon afterward intentionally destroyed their new family. I was appalled when they deliberately killed their own young. I remember the occurrence well; it was so startling to me that a mother was capable of performing such a brutal deed against her own young.

It did not, in my wildest dreams, occur to me that someday I would hear of fellow humans doing the same barbaric act to *our* offspring! Even today, so many humans choosing to terminate pregnancy by deliberately aborting seems surreal and, if it were not in fact happening, beyond belief.

Throughout history, our world faced many ugly reminders of people thinking some human brethren possessed a lesser existence, and therefore were undesirable and their presence on earth undeserved.

The right to do something does not mean that doing it is right.
—*William Safire*

It is legal in many countries to abort little ones before birth. However, if you accept the premise that your foundation for obtaining happiness and purpose comes through serving others, then you will make your own rule on this issue rather than accept the standard adopted by your government.

CHAPTER 10

YOUR SUBCONSCIOUS MIND

You are what you think. You are energy in motion, constantly adopting a new state of being. You experience mental change even at times when you seem to zone off into space from your physical surroundings or as you sleep.

Consider the thought "you are what you think" to an even deeper application: not your whole mind, and all its conscious thought, but rather your *subconscious* mind reveals the real you. From this perspective, your conscious level of thinking (your brain) now becomes another *tool* for the real you (your subconscious mind) to use. At first glance, looking at your subconscious mind as being *you* may seem like a bizarre way to view yourself.

Compare your mind's processing of thought to your body's processing of physical food. Your subconscious mind provides the "mental enzymes and catalysts" necessary for the processing of your conscious thought. These digestive juices come from two sources; the original wiring of your hard drive that was present at birth, and notions and convictions you have, by choice, placed within your subconscious mind.

It is the same with your physical body. Your health of body is affected by your own unique physical configuration as well as by what you allow to enter as food. A primary difference is the "food" entering your subconscious mind has more far-reaching consequence for you in your quest for wholeness and joy than does the food entering your body.

You allow different "truths" to filter into your subconscious mind. The "truths" in your subconscious mind range all the way from deeply buried feelings of your youth, some of which you can't even *consciously* bring to memory, right up to your accepted view of the sentence you are reading now. Subconscious thought can be compared to your physical body's configuration. There are characteristics inside your physical body you are totally oblivious to, yet they exist and affect your motion and physical action. Likewise, there are characteristics inside your subconscious mind you are totally oblivious to, yet they are there and affect how you consciously think and act.

With that, you should now have a more complete understanding of a thought presented back in chapter one: you are what you think. More specifically, what beliefs are stored in your *subconscious mind*, not your conscious thinking, expresses the real you.

You are Who You Decide to Be

The programming of your "truths" previously chosen by you for you mandates *you are as you have decided to become*.

You may say, "Now wait a minute! I didn't decide, *nor* mandate, my friend should die, my home should be destroyed by a tornado, or some maniac should impose a hideous fear on our world. None of it was my doing!"

Okay, fair enough. But you do decide what your own *reaction* to any particular occurrence will be. Occurrences are continuously happening all around you in the physical world. But of far more importance to you is what is happening in the world of your subconscious mind. Change occurs for you within your subconscious mind. Your *perception* of an occurrence or situation determines what influence the occurrence itself imparts on you, and what, if any, new "truth" you derive out of the occurrence. The physical world around you changes for you only as *your perception* changes.

> **The world we have created is**
> **a product of our thinking;**
> **it cannot be changed without**
> **changing our thinking.**
> —*Albert Einstein*

A circumstance that is considered a catastrophe to one person may be viewed as relatively insignificant to another. Any physical occurrence holds potential to hinder you, help you, or be of no consequence whatsoever to you. But the final decision of influence is always yours. You are in charge of programming your subconscious mind.

It is most unfortunate many people simply let life happen without defined direction. They wander aimlessly toward their ambiguous "goal" of wherever worldly circumstances take them.

Whether you are a derelict living on the street or you became president of the United States, you are as you choose to be. You accept certain "truths" as your own which thus far have gotten you to where you are right now. *You* are personally accountable.

And you will become in the future whatever you program yourself to be.

> **A man is but a product of his thoughts;**
> **what he thinks, that he becomes.**
> —*Mohandas K. Ghandi*

We Share Physical Similarities

Speaking of the president, or anyone else who occupies a very high level of importance in your eyes, realize this: that exalted person has striking similarities to yourself.

Picture the president's world.

His mind requires regeneration through sleep, the same as your mind does. Does he snore? With his mouth hanging half open? Do you think he sleeps soundly, or does he toss fitfully when he expects the upcoming day to be particularly stressful?

When he wakes up in the morning, your president probably does not too closely resemble the fine-looking character the cameras catch during the day. Does he have crinkly lines on his face from being scrunched against the pillow and puffy eyes just like when you first wake up? How about that morning breath?

He, like you, has to choose what clothes he's going to wear each day. "How will this outfit look when I am with so-and-so? Will photographers be around snapping photos, or can I go semi-casual today?" When he gets dressed, he does so one pant leg at a time, just like you.

When he occupies the bathroom, he very likely requires use of the exhaust fan. He needs to shave and probably uses a dose of water or gel to get that renegade wisp of hair in place.

Later in the day, he might experience gassy discomfort from choosing the wrong lunch. Hmm, I wonder what the president does when the gas pressure gets to be too much?

And his muscles experience soreness when he plays too much golf or tennis.

The point is, people considered to be of importance in this world are so very human and have similar frailties as your own. They have the same human body parts and require the same human bodily functions. Distinguished and celebrated people are not *physically* very different than yourself.

The primary difference in individuals is their *mental* nature. How and what you choose to think determines whether you excel or diminish in relation to others or in relation to your previous self.

Direct Your Thoughts

Your subconscious mind offers a most unique and useful characteristic. **Your subconscious mind can be voluntarily programmed to accept as truth *anything* you choose to feed it,** as long as the new programming is compatible with your previous programming.

This characteristic gives you the self-empowering ability to direct your own thought. We humans can appreciate the most fortunate advantage we possess over all other life on earth by the fact that only what *we allow* to enter our mind is allowed in. No other animal exists possessing the intelligent sense of reasoning to distinguish what is good "food" and what is bad "food" for the nourishment of its own mind.

You can direct your subconscious mind toward any goal of your choosing. The ability to self-direct is a quality of divine character programmed into your original hard drive.

The vast majority of humans do not come to fully realize their powerful advantage in deliberately directing subconscious thought for their own benefit. Even in this day of having so much information at your disposal, there is *still* no bit of knowledge that benefits you more than the acquisition of understanding how to manage your own subconscious mind.

> **We have guided missiles
> and misguided men.**
> —*Martin Luther King, Jr.*

The subconscious mind does not reason for itself. Reasoning occurs at the conscious level. Your subconscious mind accepts whatever your conscious mind feeds it. You can force-feed it good thoughts and new habits.

Unfortunately, feeding your subconscious mind thoughts of a negative nature works equally well. As an example, when my wife and I were newlyweds, she, being a volleyball enthusiast, decided one evening to go down to the local school gymnasium to play a few hours of open-to-the-public recreational volleyball. I ventured along. When we arrived, a game had just begun, so my wife and I watched the remainder of the game.

The thoughts running through my head as we watched were not benefiting me. "Wow! These players are really good. I can't play that well. My last recollection of playing volleyball is when I was in fourth grade elementary. As I recall, I was the worst player on both teams back then, and I haven't tried volleyball since. I cannot play nearly as well as these people."

I took the negative thought already in my subconscious mind and added even *more* reinforcement to it.

Mind is everything;
we become what we think.
—*Buddha*

When that first game was completed, we were invited to join in. How would you guess my quality of play was after all my self-talk? Things went exactly as I programmed for myself. Both the first two balls that came my way landed squarely on my chest untouched by human hands! It happened not only one time, but twice! I felt humiliated and quite embarrassed.

I must again emphasize you cannot force-feed something through the brain filter that is in disagreement with your current programming. The thought being fed to the subconscious mind needs to make sense to you at the conscious and reasoning level.

It takes repetitious prompting to create significant change in your internal programming. Past subconscious programming must be rewritten a little at a time. In the case of my volleyball embarrassment, in the weeks following, my wife and I went back again and again. With all that playing, and eventually with some actual positive examples to feed into my subconscious mind, my volleyball play did improve. That first embarrassing night occurred more than twenty-nine years ago, and I have been playing proficiently enough to enjoy the game ever since those first couple weeks.

A Tale

One evening an old Cherokee told his grandson about a battle going on inside himself.

He said, "My son, it is between two wolves. One is evil: anger, envy, sorrow, regret, greed, arrogance, self-pity, guilt, resentment, inferiority, lies, false pride, superiority, and ego.

The other is good: joy, peace, love, hope, serenity, humility, kindness, benevolence, empathy, generosity, truth, compassion, and faith."

The boy thought about it for a minute and then asked his grandfather, "Which wolf wins?"

The old Cherokee simply replied, "The one I feed."[10]

Energize the Positive

You nurture your subconscious mind through input of conscious thought. This can work for you, as well as against you. It depends on what you feed your subconscious mind.

When you force-feed positive affirmations, you program your mind to produce positive output. On the other hand, when you feed your subconscious mind thoughts of doubt or lack of belief, your results will come out negative. You attract what you think about. By worrying about some particular possibility, or complaining about something you dislike, you actually energize your mind *toward* the very thing that is bothering you. Rather than putting energy into avoiding what you don't like, try focusing on a positive expectation. In that way, you add energy to the positive possibility.

Whether positive- or negative-minded, you are the person who sets up the programming in your hard drive. You create your own self-fulfilling prophecy by how you choose to think. The outcome of what you set up is as predictable as the outcome of any computer's hard drive.

Results Come from Within

Results come from thought. Other people and occurrences may offer input but, unless you internalize the outside circumstance, that potential input has no effect on your thought. You are affected by expressions of doubt, encouragement, joy, or sorrow which develop through your own thought, and *only* your own thought.

You have absolute dominion over your conscious thought.

Real happiness is not dependent on external things...
You must cultivate your mind
if you wish to achieve enduring happiness.

—*William Lyons Phelps (paraphrased)*

Dreams are Analyzable

Dreams come to us through subconscious energy. Your dreams originate from two very exalted sources. They represent your very subconscious mind itself, or come from the Divine Creator working within your subconscious mind.

Oftentimes people experience dreams of forewarning that later come to be a reality. Clairvoyant premonitions likely come directly from the Master Creator himself. The Divine Creator communicates through openly receptive human minds. To the uninitiated mind, the phenomenon of clairvoyance may seem mysteriously bewildering, and therefore unbelievable.

Other dreams, the dreams that originate solely from within your own subconscious thinking, also carry meaning for you. Those dreams originate from your very deepest essence, the real you. Thus, the dream itself reveals a portion of your character, your makeup.

Sometimes it can be relatively easy to decipher where a dream came from, and to analyze its relevance. Other times a dream can be totally confusing and seem to make no sense at all. But be assured the dream itself came from within the essence of what *you* think on a subconscious level. There is some meaning attached to your dream's existence, whether or not you are able to explain it to yourself at the reasoning level of conscious thinking.

Hypnosis

You have been hypnotized many times in your life. Anytime you were on a road trip, as your mind wandered off, your physical presence and your mental state were quite far apart. You may not recall having passed through several towns because "you were not there." Or there have been times when someone droned on and on as you made appearances to be listening, but your mind was actually far away. You may have suddenly realized a question was being directed toward you, but you had not a clue how to answer because "you were not there." In each of those occasions, you experienced hypnotic trance.

Hypnosis is a dreamlike state of semi-consciousness. Think of directed hypnosis as "directed dreaming." While under trance, the hypnotist plants thoughts into the subconscious mind of the subject (the person being hypnotized). As long as the idea is compatible with her previous programming, the subject's subconscious mind can accept hypnotic suggestion as "truth." The suggestion thus becomes reality in her mind.

Let's say a person believes smoking is injurious and truly desires to stop smoking, and allows herself to be put into a state of hypnosis. If those conditions are met, it becomes relatively easy to plant the idea of gaining the benefit of renewed health and vigor into the subconscious mind of the hypnotized individual. The hypnotist might reiterate the already present belief that the subject desires to stop smoking, and further suggests that she *is* stopping. Possibly a repulsion of the smell of cigarette smoke can even be planted into her subconscious thinking, depending on whether she currently likes or dislikes the smell.

Hypnosis offers one way to reprogram the subconscious mind. Some people have a fear of using the tool of hypnosis. Like most fears, it derives from lack of understanding how it works.

In chapter eleven, we will look at a similar method that requires the assistance of no other person. The method explains how to *self*-direct your mind's re-programming.

Let Your Subconscious Mind Do the Work

Your subconscious mind works on solutions to problems without exertion on your part, if you permit it. However, a state of anxiety, frustration, or anger actually creates an obstruction of activity flow from your subconscious mind to your reasoning mind. By letting go of your negative emotions, you can take advantage of your subconscious mind's ability to effortlessly solve problems.

How many times have you tried thinking of a name, which just wouldn't surface for you? It seems the harder you try in these situations, the more elusive the result. Finally, in frustration, you concede and give up trying. A short time later, your subconscious mind unexpectedly throws the name out there for you.

There is a practice available to more fully commission your subconscious mind's ability to solve problems effortlessly. The mental activity your subconscious mind partakes in *as you sleep* can be directed to some extent. What you think about as you drift into a semi-conscious state right before falling asleep resides on the surface of your mind as you sleep. Your subconscious mind contemplates the subject further as your conscious mind rests.

Many times, you awaken to discover you found a solution to the problem plaguing you. Or, within a few days, the answer "miraculously" pops into your mind.

Your Mind is a Magnet

Your mind attracts what you desire. You gravitate toward whatever you think about.

If you are interested in watching birds, working with woodcrafts, or admiring classic cars, that is what you read about, talk about, and desire to learn more about. So it makes sense you will gravitate in that direction.

But, magnetic attraction toward your focus also works on a deeper level than that of a casual hobby. It works in love attraction, wealth attraction, or for *any* attainment.

What Do You See in Others?

What you see in others is a reflection of you. When you notice much of the natural world's beauty around you, it is a reflection of your own beautiful outlook.

The world is as good as you are.
—Steve McQueen

If you're a person who usually likes people even *before* you get to know them, you yourself tend to be a likable person. When you admire your paunchy husband on the couch watching his third football game of the day, it is because *you* are admirable. Conversely, when you direct angry hostility toward others, it is because you hold some anger toward yourself. Whether you have an inclination to say kind or offensive things of others, those same qualities tend to be of your own character.

You can find on the outside
only what you possess on the inside.
—Adolfo Montiel Ballesteros

If you want a happier, more fulfilling relationship with others, first work on the relationship you have with yourself. Do you hold a healthy and deserved respect for yourself? As you are able to love yourself, you become capable of loving others.

CHAPTER 11

TRANSFORMATION TOWARD YOUR DESIRES

It is sad to witness people plodding through life aimlessly and without purpose. It seems an unnecessary and senseless misuse of the fantastically wonderful gift of life. Especially since making life fun and fulfilling is a relatively simple process.

In this chapter, you learn the steps to use in a sensible, and simple, strategy that helps you acquire desires and objectives. Once you acquire the habit of using these self-help tools, you will wonder why you hadn't learned this simple methodology earlier in your life and why almost *everybody* is not making use of the procedure. It is so basic to human psychology, and so beneficial to the user, that the strategy *ought* to be included as an integral part of every elementary school's curriculum.

This is the step-by-step procedure to use in the re-programming of your subconscious mind.

One: Develop a Burning Desire

When you want to acquire something, it is certainly helpful to embrace a very strong desire for that objective. The stronger your desire, the stronger your drive for its attainment.

> **Success isn't a result of**
> **spontaneous combustion.**
> **You must set yourself on fire.**
> —*Arnold H. Glasow*

You can actually develop strong desire within yourself. The following steps will help you in intensifying your desire. However, an important caveat here: be very careful about what you elect to develop a strong desire for; be very certain what you desire is something that will benefit you.

Two: Focus on that Desire

A principal difference between an ordinary and an extraordinary person is those who are able to enjoy abundance and affluence, almost without exception, develop an ability to *focus* in an area of their lives. They learn to get good, and excel above most people's expectations, at something. Not surprisingly, their success often results in the flow (to themselves) of an abundance of respect, love, money, or other significance they find desirable.

Focusing toward what seems to be working for the benefit of your self naturally makes sense. Still, as obvious as that may seem, most people lack the wherewithal to do just that, to focus. Focusing allows you the ability to gravitate more assuredly toward your desire.

> **Only through focus**
> **can you do world-class things,**
> **no matter how capable you are.**
> —*Bill Gates*

You focus by creating a fixation on your burning desire. Give your burning desire *priority* over things of lesser importance to you. Become totally committed. Going halfway establishes a fast track to mediocrity and failure.

As you focus on your burning desire, you begin to recognize the truth "as you think is as you become."

**You can be anything you want to be,
do anything you set out to accomplish,
if you hold to that desire
with singleness of purpose.**
—*William Adams*

Don't we all have those things we start and somehow, with time, the momentum gets lost? That is, our priorities and our focus become sidetracked by other things—things that we decide are of more importance at the moment.

If you choose to ignore the power of focus, you will accomplish little with your time. You find yourself flitting from one request for attention to another. These requests may come from you or from someone else; it doesn't matter. Until you learn to focus on self-directed priorities, little consequence comes of your efforts and activity.

Vacillating people seldom succeed.
—*L.G. Elliott*

Three: Feed Affirmations

Self-talk is thought directed toward oneself, sometimes out loud, sometimes silently. Self-talk, even though it comes *from* you, is not always of a nature that is good *for* you. Self-talk, or autosuggestion, can be consciously controlled dialogue with yourself that is good for you.

Autosuggestion is an organized way to rewrite programming that needs correction in your thinking. Autosuggestion means to simply repeat affirmations of desirable statements to your own mind. To be most effective, affirmations should be used in the present tense. Use the words "I create," "I possess," or "I (active verb describing your new desirable activity)," rather than "I will be" or "I am going to." By using positive and directed affirmations, you feed your subconscious mind thoughts that persuade you toward your desired objective.

Since your Creator uses the subconscious mind as his link for communication with you, prayer directed toward your Creator and autosuggestion directed toward your own thinking become similarly operative. They both work toward the same end, and they both utilize the subconscious mind. In both instances, to be more assuredly effective, it is beneficial to pursue (pray or self-suggest) with a **sense of expectancy** and a sense of gratitude for the anticipated result.

Remember, any affirmation you use must be considered right in your conscious thinking before your subconscious mind can accept the thought. You cannot convince your subconscious mind of one thing while, at the same time, consciously think to yourself, "This affirmation is a bold-faced lie."

As an example, a person seeking financial wealth may use the words "I experience wealth and gain additional new abundance." Or if she feels she is actually in a state of lack, she may use an affirmation like "I deserve wealth. I do what is necessary to attain financial reward." But the food she feeds her subconscious mind must be in a form viewed as palatable and acceptable "truth" before it will be consumed.

Affirmations and prayers become more effective when repeated over and over again. If your surrounding conditions require, affirmations can be stated silently. However, when possible, state the affirmations aloud for greater effect. Your subconscious mind receives audible affirmations more readily.

You may also want to post the written affirmation where you see it often as a reminder. It could go on the bathroom mirror, the refrigerator, by your favorite chair in the living room, or in your car, purse, or wallet.

Since you gravitate toward that which you think about, repetitious affirmations throughout the day will be most useful to you.

Four: Visualize it

Just as everyone already uses self-talk, each of us already employs visualization as well. You can very often see an expected result in your mind before its actual physical manifestation.

Visualization, like affirmations, is a tool that many people use in a manner that is, unfortunately, detrimental to their own happiness. However, *you* can direct your visualization toward positive expectations and consequently positive results.

To direct a visual, place a picture within your mind of having *already* obtained your desire, even before its actual acquisition. Visualize yourself being where you desire to be; get a clear picture. This process works exactly like your mind does when you dream, except you pro-actively create and influence *this* dream.

Your *emotional* involvement while visualizing creates a more powerful attachment to the desired result. Close your eyes and place yourself right where you choose to be. See, smell, taste, hear, and touch the result as vividly as you can. How does your visualization make you feel? Experience emotions as if the actual attainment of your desire already exists. This emotional bond establishes a greater, more powerful impression of desire within your mind.

> **The vision that you glorify in your mind,**
> **the ideal that you enthrone in your heart –**
> **this you will build your life by,**
> **and this you will become.**
> —*James Lane Allen*

As you experience the emotion of your directed dream, you actually utilize self-hypnosis, a most useful tool for directing your mind alteration.

My father used to say that as a child he liked reading comic books about man going to the moon. In that era, the idea was so far-fetched that it made good subject matter for authors of fantasy.

Since that fantasy eventually came to be reality, obviously someone was able to visualize and feel the reality in her own mind *before* its physical occurrence. At that precise moment, the possibility of going to the moon no longer remained merely an amusing fantasy but became a new "truth" for humanity. The "impossible" began, as a thought impulse, to take form, just as the once-flat earth centuries earlier began to take its new form.

> **One's mind, once stretched by a new idea,**
> **never regains its original dimensions.**
> —*Oliver Wendell Holmes, Jr.*

Then in 1969, it happened. The reality of the possibility took its physical form. Humans actually traveled more than 200,000 miles through space and walked on the moon.

The idea had gone from impossibility, to thought, to *visualization*, and finally to its physical occurrence.

Five: Plan

A goal is much more than a wish. How is a goal different?

You can do more than simply wish for a better life for yourself. Set a *goal*. A goal is a wish with a date, and a plan, attached for its attainment. Not just "someday," but a written down, circled on the calendar, real deadline for acquisition.

Again, make sure your goal is something you really want. Your goal needs to be worth expending your time and effort on.

If the goal is *real* big, you will want to set smaller sub-goals to reach the larger end result. All the smaller sub-goals should also have dates, along with a plan for their achievement, attached to each of them. A person who sets a goal for herself of losing thirty-five pounds by a specific date, might also set incremental five-pound sub-goals, with dates attached for the attainment of each. This method becomes less daunting, and the sub-goals with deadlines, offer the added advantage of becoming a measurable guide in her progress toward her major goal.

With each sub-goal, you benefit by following all the prescribed steps. Create desire, focus, the affirmations, the visualization, and the emotional attachment.

Define your goal clearly. A goal should be very specific, measurable, and achievable. Once you define your goal and develop a plan for its attainment, get started right away. For many people, beginning can be the hardest part. It seems there is always something that needs attention before getting on with your priority. That mentality is counterproductive. Get started, just do it.

> **Whatever you can do or dream you can, begin it. Boldness has genius, power and magic in it...**
> —*Johann Wolfgang Von Goethe*

When setting goals for yourself, never choose *happiness, fun,* or *wealth* as your goal. Such goals offer no tangible measure of when you have arrived. Happiness, fun, and wealth become by-products of having achieved your goal, but they are not goals in themselves.

To come up with a goal that will result in wealth for you, ask yourself what you hope to acquire by obtaining wealth. What will wealth itself do for you? Or for hap-

TRANSFORMATION TOWARD YOUR DESIRES

piness, what *exact condition* will make you feel happy? Once you decide what will provide wealth, fun, or happiness for you, *that* objective becomes the focus of your journey. Then, you can set a measurable goal and begin laying a plan for its attainment. If you choose an appropriate goal for yourself, you may ultimately enjoy happiness, fun, or wealth.

If your objective excites you with enthusiastic joy and passion, you find immediate happiness in working toward the objective. Often you will even find the eager anticipation during the process of attainment ultimately proves to be as enjoyable as the actual arrival of the end result. Make sure the journey toward your goal remains an enjoyable experience for you.

Six: Expect Success

Possessing a confidence that you *will* receive what you are working for is an empowering condition. Expectation of a specific desirable end result creates inner drive and energy to persist. By following all the steps above, you certainly place odds very heavily in favor of acquiring your desired result, so you *should* expect success.

Seven: Be Persistent

When you discover a personal endeavor, such as a job or relationship that furnishes happiness, you are indeed fortunate. But many in such position go on to discover that good fortune may not last. It is a common malady to enjoy success only to ultimately find success can be fleeting.

Almost certainly, in time, adversity presents itself. Remembering that change is a certainty, *anticipate* the arrival of forthcoming change, and be prepared to deal with it. In trying times, you benefit from lessons learned in previous encounters with adversity.

When the disappointment of adversity does strike and you are giving consideration to abandoning your endeavor, bear in mind there exists an intangible, and significant, cost to quitting. Once you accept defeat, the pain of failure remains a permanent and negative part of your life.

A circumstance, other than adversity, that might cause one to consider abandoning an enterprise, is the human requirement of challenge and resistance to boredom. You may wish to seek out a new way of doing things simply to relieve your own boredom, even though your methods continue to work as smoothly and successfully as ever. This is a human condition that is simply built into your hard drive at birth, a condition likely designed to help keep your thinking fresh and geared toward newness. The important thing to recognize here is what is going on in your mind, and if you still find it desirable to seek change, then challenge yourself to improve, rather than merely change for the sake of change.

In any endeavor, you are naturally more likely to stay motivated and persevere by first choosing an objective you strongly desire.

Learn More on this Subject

Having read numerous developmental, self-help, and motivational books over the years of my adult life, I have happened upon many good books. In my opinion, there is one outstanding work, head and shoulders above the others. Although written decades ago, *Think and Grow Rich,* by Napoleon Hill, has become a classic for good reason, and is still widely read and studied today. I have read the distinguished work perhaps ten or twelve times, and expect to do so again in the future. It is a great study—something is picked up in each new reading. Also, re-reading the book reiterates fundamental principles of mind management that can get sidetracked as we evolve in our thinking.

If you would like to better grasp the steps and concepts involved in the attainment of your desires, I suggest you get a copy and read Napoleon Hill's explanation of the process.

Steps for Attaining Your Desires

One: Develop a burning desire

Two: Focus on that desire

Three: Feed your mind helpful affirmations

Four: Visualize and "feel" the attainment of your desire

Five: Create an incremental and measurable plan for attainment

Six: *Expect* your success!

Seven: Adversity happens, persevere

CHAPTER 12

ACQUIRING THROUGH BELIEF AND EXPECTATION

One evening my wife and I were entertaining some friends, casually relaxing in the living room of our home. In conversation, the idea of obtaining what we desire through the power of expectancy came up. When our friend mentioned it, my initial impulsive thought was everybody knows that. But within an instant, I realized that, sadly, many people are *not* aware of that phenomenon at all.

At that, I felt an impulse to write the thought down as a reminder. I did just that, although at the time I wasn't sure why. I felt a vague desire to somehow help others come to realize this profound truth and benefit by it. People should not have to learn the hard and slow way, or worse, to never come to the realization at all of this and other fundamental truths.

A moment later, the new and fragile idea of writing this book first delicately lit on the surface of my mind.

Believe With a Faith of Expectancy

It is truth that **that which you have a great desire to acquire, and believe with a faith of expectancy you *will* acquire, is yours for the taking.** That includes *any* thought, action, or physical thing.

> **As far as possibilities go,**
> **everything is possible**
> **for the person who believes.**
> —*Mark 9:23 GW*

It is a self-empowering truth I wish everyone in this world would master and claim as her own. It is a truth that is wired into the hard drive of every brain of every human being at birth, yet, for many, remains largely undeveloped. The power of believing with a faith of expectancy is little understood by the average person and is unknown to the vast majority. That is sad. It is a built-in circumstance anyone and everyone can use for their own benefit.

Train Your Mind

Since you command your physical body to do what your mind regards as fitting, it behooves you to *first* train your mind. Train your mind to accept "truths" that benefit rather than cause limitation for you. You, solely at your own discretion, allow self-growth or self-limitation.

> **Whether you believe**
> **you can do a thing or not,**
> **you are right.**
> —*Henry Ford*

Once you train your subconscious mind to expect *positive* outcome, you will find it as simple a matter to expect positive results as it was previously to expect negative results. *Whatever* your actual expectation is, your mind gravitates toward that expectancy.

Up until this very moment, you trained your mind methodically in a fashion similar to that described in this book, *or* you made it your choice to allow random chance to train your mind in a meandering and haphazard fashion. Whether or not you are willing to admit it, you are right now in your life where you have decided to be. Congratulations! I hope you arrived intentionally.

You now know, by your own self-direction, you can develop greater results for yourself as you choose. You are now armed with logical and convincing reason to *expect* your own success.

The Establishment of a New Standard

Early in the last century, common knowledge maintained it was physically impossible for any human to run a mile in less than four minutes.

But Roger Bannister was not common. He practiced with the very intent of doing the "impossible." He believed he could, and he would, beat the four-minute barrier. Bannister *expected* his own success.

In May of 1954, Bannister accomplished his goal of running the mile in under four minutes, setting a new world record. With the barrier broken, it became every runner's new paradigm—the under-four-minute mile was indeed possible. Under four minutes became the new standard to beat.

A mere month and a half later, a man by the name of John Landy broke Bannister's amazing accomplishment. In fact, within the next two years, more than *fifty* runners broke the previous barrier of four minutes!

What happened here? Why did so many new speedsters appear on the track all of a sudden? Were people training better? Well, yes, runners likely were in superior physical condition compared to what they had been previously.

But their superior physical condition came about because they first transformed their minds. Some new information penetrated through their brain filters. Virtually every brain realized it was possible for a human to run a mile in less than four minutes. And they trained their bodies according to their new belief.

> **Within you right now is the power**
> **to do things you never dreamed possible.**
> **This power becomes available to you**
> **as soon as you can change your beliefs.**
> —*Dr. Maxwell Maltz,*
> author of *Psycho-Cybernetics*

Dare to Dream Big

Every occurrence in your life, whether intentional or accidental, begins with thought.

Make your dreams meritorious dreams. Have noble thoughts. The nobility of your thought determines the richness of your life. When you choose to think worthy thoughts, your actions become worthy.

> **Aude aliquid dignum**
> —*16th century Latin phrase meaning*
> *"Dare something worthy"*

Your Beliefs Define You

Stop for just a half-minute here and think about your plans for the rest of this day. You already have a pretty good idea what the rest of your today will be like. You have probably visualized it for yourself, setting your parameters for that little portion of your future. You have given some definition as to whom you will become in that small part of your life.

What you think is who you are; what you think determines who you become in the future. You live up to your beliefs, or you live down to your beliefs.

**Just as the waves of the ocean
create distinct physical formations
of sand and rock on beaches,
the waves of our thoughts
create physical manifestations in our experience.**
—Lou Tice

Believe you were put on this earth with a purpose higher than to accept the drudgery of labor for money. And believe you were put on this earth with a purpose higher than self-gratification and self-entertainment.

Act as You Wish to Become

Once you start something, it takes hold of your thought process. Begin doing what you want to do. Just get started, get momentum going! Begin becoming what you want to become. Beginning speeds up and helps assure the successful transformation in your mind toward the new you.

If you want to be a more exciting person, get excited. If you want to enjoy more fun in your life, begin laughing more.

> **There are shortcuts to happiness, and dancing is one of them.**
> —*Vicki Baum*

If you want to be a wealthy person, stop thinking lack, and start thinking abundance. Begin to realize and appreciate the abundance you already possess at this time and truly *believe* you will further acquire wealth you desire and deserve. The change in your thought process adds momentum, helping to direct the continuation of what you have begun.

Think as if and act as if what you desire is *already* taking place, and your thought and action will assist in the desired result coming to be.

> **Think excitement, talk excitement, and you are bound to become an excited person.**
> —*Norman Vincent Peale*

I make it sound so simple. And **if you can change *the way you think*, it truly is that simple.**

Train yourself to think in a beneficial way. If you have been doing things in a non-beneficial way for twenty, thirty, or forty years, the *mental* turn toward prosperity becomes the difficult part. It takes practice and time, but once your mind *is* transformed, your desirable physical equivalent appears eagerly for you.

Physical reality manifests through thought, followed by action.

Your Own Board of Directors

Anyone claiming to be "self-made" did not make it completely on her own. No one is capable of reaching her greatest potential without the assistance of others. People who perform the greatest accomplishments in this world use other people for their *own* benefit. This fact, that accomplished individuals use other people, is not to imply they are selfish or corrupt.

> ## To the degree you give others
> ## what they need,
> ## they will give you what you need.[11]

For example, salespeople cannot earn a living without showing customers a benefit to using their product. Likewise, the consumer cannot gain without first learning how the product benefits her. If the product is purchased and performs as promised, the transaction becomes a win-win situation. Both parties used someone's assistance in order to benefit themselves.

Similarly, successful businesses usually employ a group of advisors and decision-makers. They are referred to as a company's board of directors.

Successful athletes likewise hire coaches to help direct themselves toward their desired performance.

> **If I have seen farther than other men,**
> **it is by standing**
> **on the shoulders of giants.**
> —*Isaac Newton*

Likely without even realizing it, *you* pick coaches and a board of directors for yourself. They are the people you choose to regard as your friends and mentors. These people influence decisions you make. As the most influential people in your life, they comprise your board of directors.

For most of us, picking our board of influential people is a haphazard occurrence. Little, if any, conscious thought goes into it. It just happens without deliberate consideration.

Is your board of directors good for you? Is your board of directors working to your benefit? If not, fire them. Each of your friends is replaceable, and, if they are not good for you, then they *should* be replaced.

When you are in crisis, it is difficult to make sound and rational decisions. At such times, you tend to magnify certain aspects of your current little picture. When not in control of your senses, it becomes easy to lose sight of the big picture, thereby blocking your ability to be objective and rational in decision-making. If you cultivate a good board of directors for yourself, your board helps you navigate through difficult times with minimal loss.

Surround yourself with the support of people who help you. Surround yourself with positive-oriented and successful people and glean positive rewards through your friendships.

In addition to your circle of influential family and friends, there is another idea you may wish to consider. In *Think and Grow Rich*, Napoleon Hill has a chapter entitled "Power of the Master Mind."

I, no doubt, do Mr. Hill an injustice here by trying to paraphrase his concept of the Master Mind counsel. But the substance of the Master Mind concept is to set up, within your own mind, a group of people you revere as being wise counsel. The group may consist of people you know. It can even be people you do not personally know, or maybe famous people from the past who were revered for possessing wisdom in a certain area of life that is relevant to you.

There is a most noteworthy alliance of historic characters who were influenced by great mentors.

In ancient Athens, Socrates was regarded as a great teacher and philosopher of his time. He became respected as an educator who was primarily interested in helping people to find the good within themselves.

One of his students, Plato, went on to great accomplishments of his own. Plato eventually built, and was himself a greatly respected teacher in, the great Academy of Athens.

Aristotle, one of Plato's pupils at the Academy, grew up to become regarded as "probably the most scholarly and learned of the ancient Greek philosophers."[12] Besides earning acclaim as a renowned philosopher, Aristotle was also an educator and scientist. He, too, founded his own school, naming it the Lyceum.

The meritorious Alexander the Great received part of his education at the Lyceum. Alexander the Great went on to conquer all of Greece and overthrew the Persian Empire. He built and ruled an impressive empire of his own before his premature death at the age of thirty-three years.

All these people received influence from great mentors. Each is regarded with veneration in our history books even twenty-three centuries later.

A rather remarkable succession of great mentors and students!

> **The mediocre teacher tells.**
> **The good teacher explains.**
> **The superior teacher demonstrates.**
> **The great teacher inspires.**
> —*William Arthur Ward*

It makes one wonder if perhaps the Academy and the Lyceum taught a little more than reading, writing, and arithmetic, doesn't it? Academics are necessary tools as far as life's *basic* skills go. However, it seems these students acquired something more than the normal appropriation of academic facts. Consider each of these individual's revered status of high regard by others (both in their contemporary time and centuries later) and the common interlace of association with each other. One might speculate this impressive list of distinguished educators and philosophers were each being stimulated with some uncommonly useful fundamental principles that go beyond traditional education—beneficial principles not accepted by the common majority.

> **There are obviously two educations.**
> **One should teach us**
> **how to make a living**
> **and the other how to live.**
> —*James Truslow Adams*

These four influential men were practiced in utilizing the concept of the Master Mind through their association with each other, although they probably did not use the term Master Mind.

Live Right Now

Your life here on earth has a beginning and will someday have an ending. What you choose to do in between the two points determines whether you live a worthy life or an ordinary life of wishing and hoping.

Sometimes we get so caught up in the little things of life that we forget to enjoy today. Many people make a habit of being burdened by relatively inconsequential matters. Meanwhile, life is passing them right by.

> **Yesterday is a cancelled check;**
> **tomorrow is a promissory note;**
> **today is ready cash – use it.**
> —*Kay Lyons*

This moment is all you *really* have. What you experience in this moment is fleeting in its nature. Whether you feel happy, sad, motivated, lazy, attractive, ugly, victorious, defeated—it is *all* temporary. It will change.

If you appreciate this moment, and the next moment, and the next, pretty soon you will have enjoyed a good day. And if you enjoy today, and tomorrow, and the next tomorrow, and you keep doing that, someday you will have lived a wonderful life. One moment at a time, one day at a time.

Remember how you spend your days is how you spend your life.[13]

In chapter three, I noted that most little moments generally do not bear any particular relevance in your big picture. While that is true, it is still important to live most of your little moments enjoyably and to the benefit of you and the world you occupy.

Each step you take becomes a step on the path either toward, or away from, the ultimate reward you seek. If you choose to waste too many moments, your pursuit of fulfillment and joy can be lost to lack of meaningful direction. This moment in time, once squandered, remains lost forever with no chance of recovery.

Live right now. Add richness to *this* moment in your life so you can appreciate this moment for what it offers.

We do not remember days, we remember moments.

—*Cesare Pavese*

CHAPTER 13

STARTING OVER

Disciplines to Live By

1. Make serving your Creator and your fellow humans the primary purpose of your life. An attitude of servitude to others and an appreciation of others guarantees your happiness.

2. Trust your Creator. Trust he will provide what is to your greatest benefit. You don't always know what is best, but trust that he does. Rather than solicit a specific occurrence, prayerfully request of him that which is most beneficial for your good and the good of all.

3. Believe in the goodness of human beings.

4. Base living your life of abundant joy on the fundamental beliefs:

    God created man in his image; in the divine image he created him.

    —*Genesis 1:27 NAB*

    Life is a daring adventure or nothing at all.

    —*Helen Keller*

    There is no security in this world, only opportunity.

    —*General Douglas MacArthur*

5. Stay young until you die by continually learning new things throughout your entire life.

6. Realize no matter what happens, your thought—and your thought alone—determines your happiness. Happiness is not the result of what happens to you but rather the result of what you choose to think. Happiness flows from the inside outward and not the other way around.

7. Keep your brain filter in a receptive-to-positive-input condition that stimulates benefit for you. You continually control your thought by filtering which beliefs become programmed into your mind. Quality in—quality out.

8. Realize your mind is trainable. Your subconscious mind becomes either your most powerful ally or your greatest enemy, depending on how you apply its use.

9. Believe you were placed on this earth deliberately and with noble purpose—a purpose higher than self-entertainment and higher than the drudgery of boring and dissatisfying work. See #1 above.

10. Take an active role in the development, direction, and positive growth of your own life. Living is not a spectator sport.

11. Learn to forgive mistakes and to let go. This grants you permission to move forward.

12. Choose optimism. Expect good things to happen. Expect your own success. You will find less disappointment and more appreciation.

Treat Life as an Adventurous Game

The disciplines detailed in this book for training, and more fully utilizing, your mind might imply much seriousness and a need to put forth your absolutely greatest effort. However, if you truly are going to enjoy life in an adventurous sense, you cannot take life all too seriously. Treat life as a game, for it is. At the same time, though, you should play the game to win.

This game is better than any card game, or board game, or children's frolic. You see, in this game of *Life*, while not everybody will win, there are indeed many, many winners. But the best rule of this game is through winning, you actually *help others* win. And, when others live a robust and fulfilling life, they win, and you benefit through their winning.

> ### True success always affects people far beyond the one who has achieved it.
> —*Chris Widener*

Although not everyone will win, *anyone* can. Everyone who chooses to win does win!

It's Your Birthday!

You were brought into this world with a brain wired for greatness. As you developed, well-intentioned friends and family members emphatically pointed out to you what you could not do. Or rather, what they *thought* you could not, or should not, do. If you were like most toddlers, one of the very first words that came out your mouth was an emphatic *NO*!

> **Our world is unreasonably negative.**
> **People are frequently put down,**
> **told what they can't do instead of**
> **what they can do.**
> —*Zig Ziglar*

The concept of negativity was hammered home enough that you eventually began to accept the new "fact" in your mind—your dreams are to be stifled. It became one of your "truths." You ultimately accepted the path of other people's expectations right down the road of mediocrity. It's a common road to travel—*too* common.

If that is the path you accepted in the past, your life may have been anything *except* a daring adventure thus far. But your past is not your future and is inter-related only to the degree you make them so. By now you surely know, no matter where you have been, your life in the future need *not* be anything less than a daring adventure.

Just one second ago, you finished the first part of your life. That is behind you, and nothing can change it. Realize, this is the very first day, the very beginning of the last apportionment of your life. With that in mind, think of today as your new birth. No matter how your self-esteem has been affected by your upbringing, and subsequent events in your life, you have complete power to move on and to change any of it. You are now presented the gift of opportunity for a brand new start for yourself. How exhilarating!

It's time to start living
the life you've imagined.
—Henry James

You enjoy some major and exciting advantages in this last portion of your life over the first. You do not need to spend fifteen to twenty-five years learning the basics. This time, they're *already* wired in. You will save an incredible effort, and considerable time, by not having to repeat that tedious task. You are ready to roll!

This time, right away on this first day, you can believe and understand the fundamentals of higher living portrayed in this book that go carelessly unconsidered in many lives, as they perhaps did in your own first apportionment. This time, you can begin immediately in training your subconscious mind to cultivate whatever life you choose for yourself.

Think of yourself as
on the threshold
of unparalleled success.
—Andrew Carnegie

Don't you dare accept anything less than an adventure for yourself!

I bargained with life for a penny,
And life would pay no more,
However I begged at evening
When I counted my scanty score.
For life is a just employer,
He gives you what you ask.
But once you have set the wages,
Why, you must bear the task.
I worked for a menial's hire,
Only to learn dismayed,
That any wage I had asked of Life
Life would have willingly paid.

—*Jessie B. Rittenhouse* 1918
from *The Door of Dreams*

NOTES

CHAPTER THREE

1. Cerf, Christopher, and Victor Navasky. 1998. *The Experts Speak*. New York: Villard.

CHAPTER FOUR

2. Croce, Pat. 2002. *110%: 110 Strategies for Feeling Great Every Day*. Simon and Schuster.

3. ibid.

4. Rohn, Jim. 1994. *The Treasury of Quotes*. Health Communications.

CHAPTER SIX

5. The World Book Encyclopedia. 1986 ed., s.v. "learning."

6. Croce, Pat. 2002. 110%: *110 Strategies for Feeling Great Every Day*. Simon and Schuster

CHAPTER EIGHT

7. Author unknown. 2003. Entrepreneurial Investing. *financialmentor.com*. (February 24, 2003)

8. McWilliams, John-Roger and Peter. 1991. *Life 101: Everything We Wish We Had Learned In School—But Didn't*. Prelude Press.

9. This example assumes a 12 percent annual return-on-investment.

CHAPTER TEN

10. Used with permission. *www.quickinspirations.com/stories/wolves.asp*. (10/17/2002)

CHAPTER TWELVE

11. Conklin, Robert. 1997. *Be Whole!*. Clifftop Publishing.

12. The World Book Encyclopedia, 1986 ed., s.v. "Aristotle."

13. Author Unknown. 2003. Capsule Sermons. *The Furrow* magazine, (fall).